CONTENTS

LES DAMES D'ESCOFFIER

The Honolulu Chapter of Les Dames d'Escoffier is part of Les Dames d'Escoffier International, a worldwide society of professional women of high achievement in the fields of food, fine beverage and hospitality. Members include chefs, bakers, restaurateurs, caterers, educators, writers, publicists, hoteliers, wine merchants, dietitians, food merchants, manufacturers, purveyors and others in the culinary world.

The Honolulu Chapter was founded in 2000. Its members are dedicated to advancing professional achievement through educational programs and community service endeavors—for example, luncheons hosted for elementary school students to teach etiquette and the art of fine dining. In 2002, the Honolulu Chapter established the Heather Ho Culinary Collection of books in the libraries of Hawai'i's seven community colleges, in memory of pastry chef Heather Ho, a victim of the terrorist attacks on September 11, 2001.

In 2006, Les Dames d'Escoffier International established a Green Tables initiative for all its chapters, a project to support civic agriculture and sustainability in communities. The Honolulu Chapter chose to coordinate the publication of this Farmers Market Cookbook as its Green Tables project.

Chapter members are Wanda Adams, Ruth Arakaki, Shawn "Possie" Badham, Cathy Smoot Barrett, Barbara Campbell, Kusuma Cooray, Soleil Fusha, Beverly Gannon, Sabine Glissmann, Holly Hadsell-El Hajji, Barbara Holm, Jean W. Hull, Elisabeth Ann Iwata, Nina Rica Jarrett, Donna Jung, Peggy King, Sharon Kobayashi, Melanie Kosaka, Noreen Lam, Abigail Langlas, Kellie Learmont, Hayley Matson-Mathes, Jo McGarry, Ivy Nagayama, Wendy Nakamura, Michelle Nakaya, Joan Namkoong, Carol Nardello, Olelo pa'a Faith Ogawa, Shannon Piper, Rebecca Schillaci, Robbyn Shim, Diana Shitanishi, Teresa Shurilla, Barbara Stange, Nancy Thomas, Cheryl To, Kay Tokunaga, Fern Tomisato, Maria Tucker, Letitia (Tish) Uyehara, Juli Umetsu, Lori Ann Wong and Linda Yamada.

FOREWORD

As president of the Hawai'i Farm Bureau Federation, it's my privilege to present this *Hawai'i Farmers Market Cookbook* to the community—a book that reflects the varied products and hard work of our state's agricultural community.

The HFBF was organized in 1948 by a group of Windward O'ahu farmers. Formally incorporated in 1950, HFBF today consists of 1,600 member families in 10 county chapters throughout the state of Hawai'i. HFBF is a not-for-profit organization dedicated to analyzing the problems affecting farming families and formulating action to ensure the future of agriculture and promoting the well-being of farming and the State's economy. Members voice their ideas and opinions at the county level, and policies are adopted at county and state meetings. HFBF is an active lobbyist in the State Legislature, especially on issues of land use and water. Marketing programs and the role of agriculture in the state's economy and social structure are also important to HFBF and its members.

The *Hawai'i Farmers Market Cookbook* has been a dream of mine ever since we opened the Kapi'olani Community College Farmers Market in 2003. A big thank you goes to the members of the Honolulu chapter of Les Dames d'Escoffier for taking this book on as a project for HFBF and doing literally all the work of gathering, testing and editing the recipes, as well as providing photography. Without them this book would not have happened.

Thank you, too, to the Hawai'i State Department of Agriculture, the College of Tropical Agriculture and Human Resources, University of Hawai'i at Mānoa and, of course, all the county chapters of HFBF for their contributions to this book. And last but not least, mahalo to the staff of HFBF, which tirelessly works to move our organization forward.

I hope this book will not only put delicious food on your table but better connect you to our local growers, so that agriculture in Hawai'i will continue to play an important role in our community.

Aloha,

Dean Okimoto
President
Hawai'i Farm Bureau Federation

HAWAI'I AGRICULTURE, ISLAND BY ISLAND

Kaua'i

The county of Kaua'i is a 555-square-mile tropical paradise, home to some 62,000 people. Its moderate climate and varied terrain produce landscapes ranging from Waimea Canyon, the "Grand Canyon of the Pacific," to Mount Waialeale, the wettest spot on earth. Kaua'i hosts one of two remaining sugar plantations in Hawai'i and the largest coffee and guava plantations in the U.S. The dry Waimea-Kekaha plain is host to seed corn that is planted and grown in the Midwest. The Hanalei Valley produces roughly two-thirds of the taro for the state's poi industry. Tropical flowers and exotic fruit like atemoya, rambutan, mangosteen, lychee and longan are grown on Kaua'i. And the red-

fleshed Sunrise papaya is unique to Kaua'i. Beef cattle and pigs are also nourished on the Garden Isle.

Maui County

The county of Maui encompasses the islands of Maui, Lana'i and Moloka'i. Central Maui is home to the state's largest remaining sugar plantation, Hawaiian Commercial and Sugar Company. In Upcountry Maui, sweet Kula onions are grown, as well as a host of vegetables like broccoli, cauliflower and cabbage. Here, too, are dozens of small farms that pro-

duce an exciting array of products like strawberries, asparagus, baby lettuces, lavender and goat cheese. Pineapple is another significant crop in upland and West Maui. Cattle ranchers also play an important role in the agricultural scene on Maui. Protea is prolific here, too, as are a host of other tropical flowers.

O'ahu

Two of the state's largest farms are on O'ahu, producing such basic items as cabbage, tomatoes, green peppers, Asian greens, melons, sweet onions, corn, bananas and squashes. Hundreds of small farmers supply cucumbers, eggplant, green onions, watercress, tomatoes, green beans, papaya, asparagus and dozens of other edibles to the densely populated island. The HFBF farmers markets are especially popular on O'ahu, where they showcase Island-grown fruits, vegetables, beef and flowers to a savvy consumer base.

The Island of Hawai'i

The Big Island is known for its cattle ranches, thousands of acres of verdant green land devoted to grazing beef cattle and lamb. Coffee in the Kona area and macadamia nuts, papayas, orchids and anthuriums in the area around Hilo are some of the largest export items in the state. In between are hundreds of farms producing ginger, citrus fruit, tomatoes, bananas, cabbages, broccoli, celery and various lettuces and cooking greens. Unique hearts of palm, vanilla, rambutan, dragon fruit, mangosteen, breadfruit, cacao and dozens of other exotic fruits and vegetables are sprouting on this island of varying landscapes and climate that can play host to almost every imaginable crop.

FARMERS MARKETS FROM KCC TO KONA

Evolution of a Community Event

In September 2003, farmer Dean Okimoto and food writer Joan Namkoong coordinated the first Saturday Farmers Market at Kapi'olani Community College on the slopes of Diamond Head. With more than 30 vendors of fresh Hawai'i-grown fruits, vegetables, flowers, beef, other agricultural products and prepared foods, this weekly event quickly became the state's premier farmers market. Primarily serving East Honolulu, the KCC market is a Saturday morning institution for the community, where coffee and breakfast are served and the freshest of Hawai'i foods are available for purchase. Kapi'olani Community College is the market's co-sponsor.

In September 2004, HFBF, with the support of Kaneohe Ranch Co. and the H.L. Castle Foundation, opened the Kailua Thursday Night Market in Kailua town. Another community institution was soon established, as Windward O'ahu residents headed to the market to purchase fresh produce or pick up hot dinners prepared by a variety of vendors.

The Mililani Farmers Market opened in March 2005 with the cooperation of Mililani High School. The Sunday morning market is a regular stop for many residents of the area.

In December 2005, the Kona County Farm Bureau, with the support of Kamehameha Schools and Keauhou Shopping Center, opened the Keauhou Farmers Market, held on Saturday mornings. Kona farmers find an eager audience of customers to purchase their varied offerings.

The HFBF farmers markets provide a way for local farmers to sell their products. All of these products must be Hawai'i grown and produced; no mainland produce or flowers are allowed. This ensures that consumers enjoy local growers' freshest and finest products and helps preserve sustainable agriculture as a vital part of the Island lifestyle.

Six Reasons to Shop at a Farmers Market

1. When you shop at a farmers market, you're getting fresher fruits and vegetables. Instead of buying produce shipped 2,500 miles over a weeklong period, you're getting

fresh food harvested within a day or two of the market. Not only will it last longer in your refrigerator, it is also more nutritious.

2. Farmers markets in Hawai'i are a wonderful mirror of the ethnic diversity of the Islands, offering a wide array of fresh locally grown choices. You'll find unique, interesting and seasonal foods at farmers markets that will broaden your horizons and cooking experiences in a healthy way.

3. By shopping at a farmers market you're supporting local farmers and their families. Your dollars help to perpetuate a vital part of our state's economy.

4. Your support of local farmers and agriculture helps to preserve agricultural lands. The greenbelt enhances Hawai'i's natural beauty. What's more, agriculture helps to replenish the water supply. When water from irrigated fields percolates into the aquifers, it provides much-needed high-quality water.

5. Supporting local farmers and buying their products helps sustain the state's economy, rather than relying on the importing of basic foods.

6. Farmers markets are just plain fun. They're places for people to meet their neighbors, to trade recipes, to catch up on the latest gossip. It's a great opportunity to learn about farming and agriculture and where your food comes from.

Hours and Locations

O'ahu
Kailua Thursday Night
Farmers Market
Thursdays, 5 p.m.-7:30 p.m.
Kailua Town Center near Longs

Saturday Farmers Market at KCC
Saturdays, 7:30 a.m.-11 a.m.
Kapi'olani Community College
4303 Diamond Head Road

Mililani Sunday Farmers Market
Sundays, 8 a.m.-noon
Mililani High School
95-1200 Meheula Parkway

Big Island of Hawai'i
Keauhou Farmers Market
Saturdays, 8 a.m.-noon
Keauhou Shopping Center
Keauhou

TIPS FOR SHOPPING AT A FARMERS MARKET

- Wear comfortable flat shoes for walking during your market adventure.

- For best selection, shop early. But if you're an early shopper, expect to wait in lines.

- HFBF farmers markets are cash markets. Bring cash in small denominations.

- Carry a reusable shopping bag or shopping basket. A cart on wheels can be handy; papayas, pineapple and other purchases can get very heavy.

- Have a cooler in your car to store perishables for the ride home.

- Buy seasonal items when you see them.

- Get to know the farmers and ven dors at the market. Ask questions and learn about their products and how they're grown.

- Check the HFBF website (www. hfbf.org) weekly for upcoming specials and events at each farm-ers market. Or call (808) 848-2074 for more information.

Hawai'i Farm Bureau Federation
2343 Rose St.
Honolulu, HI 96819
www.hfbf.org

ISLAND PRODUCTS FROM A-Z

Before you head to one of HFBF's farmers markets—or if you've just returned from one with an armload of fresh goodies—peruse the recipes in this book for some great ideas on preparing your purchases. The book is arranged in alphabetical order by the name of the product, but you'll also want to check the following listing, as well as the Index beginning on page 176, since many of the recipes use more than just a single Island-grown product.

Ahi	Fennel	Negi
Arugula	Ginger	Onions
Asparagus	Goat cheese	Oranges
Atemoya	Green beans	Papaya
Avocado	Green onion	Parsley
Bananas	Green pepper	Passion fruit
Basil	Guava	Persimmon
Beef	Habañero chili	Pineapple
Beets	Hearts of palm	Pork
Bean sprouts	Honey	Portuguese sausage
Breadfruit	Jicama (chop suey yam)	Radish
Broccoli	Kale	Salad greens
Broccoli rabe	Lamb	Soursop
Cabbage	Lemon	Soybeans
Celery	Lemongrass	Spinach
Cherimoya	Liliko'i	Strawberries
Chili	Lime	Sugar, raw
Chocolate	Lotus root	Sweet potato
Cilantro	Lychee	Swiss chard
Citrus	Macadamia nut oil	Taro
Coconut	Macadamia nuts	Tofu
Coffee	Mahimahi	Tomato
Collard greens	Mango	Turmeric
Cooking greens	Melon	Vanilla
Corn	Mint	Watercress
Cucumber	Moya	Won bok
Daikon	Mushrooms	Zucchini
Eggplant	Mustard greens	

ASPARAGUS

A sparagus reached America in the mid-17th century from Italy, and now, two centuries later, the United States is the leading producer of asparagus. Asparagus is a member of the lily family and is also related to onions and leeks. The shoots are forced to grow tall to produce a spear rather than developing branches and leaves. Spears come up either thick or thin; they do not thicken as they grow. So thickness is not a good guide to freshness.

Asparagus is highly perishable and therefore best when purchased soon after harvest. When choosing asparagus, look for compact and firm tips, smooth bright green skin, and stem ends that aren't dried out and shriveled. Thicker stems are more succulent and are easier to not overcook. Fresh asparagus has few fibers and can be eaten from bottom to top.

To store asparagus, store them like flowers. Trim the stalks and place in an inch or two of water. Cover tips with plastic or a wet paper towel to keep them moist.

Young asparagus is sweet and can be eaten raw. Cook asparagus quickly to retain the bright green color and a little of its crispness.

Asparagus Soup with Negi
Cheryl To, PacifiKool

1	pound asparagus, trimmed and cut into 2-inch pieces
2	tablespoons butter
1	small negi,* rough-chopped
1	quart chicken broth
1	medium-size potato, cut into 1-inch cubes
3	cloves roasted garlic, skin removed**
1	bay leaf
	Salt and white pepper to taste

In a soup pot over medium heat, melt the butter. Add the negi and cook, stirring constantly so it does not brown or burn. After a few minutes, when the negi is no longer opaque, add the chicken broth and bring to a boil. Add the potato, roasted garlic and bay leaf. Lower heat and simmer the soup until the potatoes start to soften. Add the asparagus and cook for a few minutes.

As soon as the asparagus cooks (it should still be bright green), remove from stove. Cool soup slightly, remove bay leaf, then puree in a blender or use a hand blender. Add salt and pepper to taste. Garnish with small pieces of asparagus or with croutons. Serve immediately.

Serves 6.

*Negi is a large Japanese green onion resembling a leek. It is grown on O'ahu's North Shore and can be found at Asian food markets.

**To roast garlic, cut a slit in the skin of the garlic cloves. Lay the cloves on a piece of foil and drizzle with a little olive oil. Bake them for approximately 20 minutes in a 350° F oven. The cloves are done when they are just brown around the edges, have a nice fragrance and smash easily.

Grilled Asparagus
Barbara Stange, Alan Wong's

1   pound asparagus

MARINADE

½   cup olive oil
½   cup balsamic vinegar
½   cup freshly squeezed orange juice
2   cloves of garlic, peeled and smashed
5   basil leaves, cut into julienne
    Freshly ground black pepper

Combine all the marinade ingredients in a container large enough to hold the asparagus. Marinate asparagus for 1-2 hours at room temperature. When ready to grill, remove from marinade and dry off excess marinade. Grill over low heat until crisp-tender. Remove and serve immediately. Marinade can be made ahead of time, refrigerated and used more than once. Serves 4.

Asparagus Risotto
Jean W. Hull, CCE

½   pound asparagus, cut into 1-inch pieces
1   tablespoon butter
1   tablespoon olive oil
3   tablespoons red onion, diced
1½ teaspoons garlic, minced
1   cup arborio rice
2¼ cups low-sodium, no-MSG chicken broth, heated
½   teaspoon salt and pepper
½   cup grated Parmesan cheese
½   cup minced parsley

Heat butter and olive oil in a large, heavy skillet over medium-high heat. Add onion and garlic and sauté until translucent, about 2 minutes. Add rice, stirring until grains are opaque, about 3 minutes. Add chicken broth, ½ cup at a time. Stir with each addition until the broth is absorbed before adding more. Continue adding broth ½ cup at a time.

With the last addition of broth, add the asparagus, salt and pepper. Taste the rice – it should be firm to the bite. Add additional both, if required, to ensure that the texture is creamy. To finish the dish, fold in Parmesan cheese and parsley. Combine and serve immediately.

Serves 4.

Asparagus Milanese
Ivy Nagayama, d.k. Steak House

1   pound asparagus
4   eggs
4   teaspoons truffle oil
1   teaspoon Italian breadcrumbs
     Salt and pepper

Trim asparagus ends. Blanch asparagus until crisp-tender. Drain well and divide among 4 plates.

In a skillet, heat a little olive oil and fry eggs sunny-side up, seasoning with salt and pepper. Place one egg on top of each plate of asparagus. Drizzle with truffle oil and sprinkle with breadcrumbs. Serve immediately.

Serves 4.

AVOCADO

The avocado also known as the alligator pear because of the texture of its skin. It is grown commercially on the Island of Hawai'i. The Sharwill is the most prized among hundreds of varieties grown in the Islands. Avocado is classified as a fruit, and, with the exception of the olive, no other fruit contains as large a percentage of fat.

Avocados fully ripen only after they have been picked from the tree. Leave avocados on your kitchen counter until you feel them give when you gently squeeze them. To help it ripen, put an avocado in a brown paper bag, close it and leave it in a dark, cool area of your kitchen. Check daily. After ripening, an avocado can be stored in the refrigerator until ready to use, though its texture may suffer. To freeze an avocado, first mash or puree it. To each cup of puree add 1½ tablespoons sugar and two teaspoons lemon juice and make a smooth paste. Pack in freezer bags or containers and freeze immediately. Depending on ripeness, you can store avocadoes up to two weeks in the refrigerator.

To prepare a fresh avocado, cut it in half. Hold the half with the seed in your hand with a towel. Remove seed by embedding knife blade into it and twisting to lift seed out. To remove flesh, run your knife around the edge of the skin. Peel off the skin and slice, dice, or mash. Avocado will start to turn color unless lemon or lime juice is added to it.

Layered California-Style Pan Sushi
Lori Wong, Culinary Consultant

This interpretation of our much-beloved California roll is easy to prepare for potluck dinners or an appetizer party.

4   cups cooked, steamed medium-grain white rice
½   cup Japanese rice vinegar
½   cup granulated sugar
1   teaspoon Hawaiian salt
½   cup mayonnaise
1   teaspoon prepared wasabi
8   ounces crab meat or surimi crab, chopped
1   whole avocado, skinned, seeded and diced
½   medium cucumber, partially skinned and diced
3   ounces tobiko, optional
2-3 packages dried seasoned nori or sushi sheet nori cut into quarters

Boil rice vinegar, sugar and salt until sugar dissolves. Cool. Gently mix the sauce into the rice with a wooden paddle while the rice is still hot. Let the rice mixture cool.

Mix mayonnaise and wasabi together. Add the crab and avocado and blend.

In a 9-inch x 13-inch glass dish spread rice in a layer. Top with crab mixture, avocado, cucumber and tobiko. To serve, spoon the layered California sushi mixture onto a nori sheet and roll.

Serves 12.

Avocado Tempura
Lori Wong, Culinary Consultant

Cooked avocado has a nutty flavor and creamy texture—but if overcooked, it may become bitter.

2   whole avocados, peeled and seeded, sliced into ½-inch thick slices
1   package tempura mix
    Vegetable oil for frying
    Salt

Follow directions on your favorite tempura mix to make 1 cup of bat-ter. Add water to thin it to the consistency of pancake batter.

Heat about 2 inches of vegetable oil in a skillet. Test to see whether it is ready by putting a few drops of tempura batter into the oil; batter should sizzle.

Dip the avocado into the batter and coat completely. Place into the cooking oil and cook until golden brown, turning if necessary. Drain on paper towels and salt. Serve immediately.

Serves 4.

Awesome Avocado Sandwich

Lori Wong, Culinary Consultant

2   whole avocados, peeled, seeded and sliced into ½-inch slices
8   slices bread
1   vine-ripened tomato, sliced thin
2   large white or red radishes, sliced thin
½   medium cucumber, semi-peeled and sliced into thin rounds
1   ounce arugula or spicy mixed greens
     Favorite salad dressing
     Salt and pepper

Place bread slices side by side (top and bottom). On the bottom slices, place tomato slices to cover the bread. Top with radish slices. Top radishes with cucumber slices. Lightly season with salt and pepper to taste.

Lightly toss the arugula or spicy greens in the salad dressing.

Top cucumber slices with dressed greens. Top with 3 slices of avocado. Season with salt and pepper.

Top with top slice of bread. Place two frilled toothpicks on opposite sides and slice in half.

Serves 4.

BANANAS

There are many varieties of bananas grown in Hawai'i, including Williams, Lady Finger, and the cooking bananas known as plantains. The favorite "table" banana in Hawai'i, however, is the pleasantly tart-sweet apple banana. Although available all year, peak production for apple bananas is November through January.

Bananas are high in iron and potassium and may help reduce the risk of high blood pressure and stroke. In addition, bananas contain tryptophan, a mood-enhancing protein, and fiber – and we all know how important fiber is.

Richard Ha, Mauna Kea Banana Co.
Hāmākua Coast, Hawai'i

For Richard Ha of Mauna Kea Banana Co., the up- and down-sides of farming are inseparable. If the down-side is that something will always go wrong, the up-side is the fun of anticipating failure, and perhaps outfoxing it. Ha, who farms nearly 600 acres on the Hāmākua Coast, says that with an agricultural operation of his size, planning is essential. " It's kind of like steering an ocean liner. We have to start turning the ship early if we see something ahead or we're not going to be able to stop," he says.

Despite its name, Mauna Kea Banana Co. is diversified, encompassing not only fields of Williams and apple bananas, but hydroponically grown tomatoes, cucumbers and baby lettuces sold under the Hamakua Springs brand. Diversifying is a family tradition. The Has originally raised chickens, but in the '60s they began trading chicken manure for banana keiki and planting out unused acres. By the '70s, they were exclusively a banana operation, but in the '90s, concerned about the threat of the bunchy top virus, Ha added the hydroponic gardens.

Today, Ha's daughter and son-in-law work in the business. Chef Alan Wong is a marketing partner, visiting the farm for tours, offering advice on what chefs and consumers want, and even cooking for employees. Ha says this has helped show his employees that the job is not just packing stuff in a box: "It's made them more conscious of what happens at the other end."

Apple Banana Tarte Tatin
Sharon Kobayashi, Latitude 22

This recipe elevates the common apple banana to elegant simplicity. Avoid using Williams or other large varieties, as they do not have the texture or flavor required for this dish. Serve with slightly sweetened whipped cream or ice cream.

2   tablespoons butter
½   cup brown sugar, packed
8   apple bananas, ripe, cut in half lengthwise
1   sheet frozen puff pastry, defrosted
    or refrigerated pie dough trimmed to fit pan
    Ground cinnamon to taste

Preheat oven to 400° F.

In a large skillet, melt 1 tablespoon of butter over medium heat. Sauté half the bananas until golden brown; remove from heat and sauté the rest, using the remaining butter.

Spray an 8-inch x 8-inch baking pan with cooking spray and then sprinkle evenly with sugar. Lay bananas over sugar, arranging in rows. Sprinkle with cinnamon. Lay pastry over, tucking edges under. Bake until pastry is golden brown, about 15-20 minutes.

Remove from oven. Cool slightly, then invert tart onto platter. Cut into 4 squares, and cut each square diagonally, forming triangles. Serve warm with vanilla ice cream or a dollop of whipped cream.

Serves 4.

Banana Curry Sauce with Fresh Turmeric
Sharon Kobayashi, Latitude 22

Fresh turmeric, also known as olena, has a delicate, earthy, peppery and floral aroma. To use fresh turmeric, wash thoroughly and peel off tough pieces of the skin. Use a ginger grater to grate. Turmeric will stain yellow, so protect your hands with plastic wrap. Transfer grated turmeric to the pot using the same piece of wrap. Store "end pieces" in a zip lock bag in the freezer, than add to any soup, as you would ginger.

4   apple bananas, cut into ½-inch dice
1   tablespoon olive oil
2   onions cut into ¼-inch dice, about 3 cups
1   tablespoon ginger, finely minced
4   cloves garlic, minced
2   tablespoons cumin, ground
1   teaspoon coriander seed, ground
2   (14-ounce) cans beef, vegetable or chicken broth
2   tablespoons fresh turmeric, grated, or 2 teaspoons dry
2   pounds vegetable and/or meat, such as ground beef or lamb, tofu,
    horenso spinach, won bok or other greens.

Preheat a large skillet on medium high heat. Add oil and onions. Reduce heat to medium and sauté onions until deep brown, about 15 minutes. Add ginger, garlic, cumin and coriander to pan and sauté about 1 minute.

Add broth and stir to release brown bits at the bottom of the pan into the sauce. Add turmeric and bananas; bring to a boil. If using beef or lamb, brown in a skillet before adding to curry. Reduce heat to a simmer and cook until bananas are tender, about 15 minutes. Add water as needed to keep a sauce-like consistency. Serve with rice.

Serves 4-6.

BEEF

Beef cattle have been a part of the agricultural landscape since 1793, when the first cows arrived at Kawaihae on the Big Island. But it wasn't until the 1830s that the beef cattle industry really got organized, when Spanish vaqueros taught Hawaiians how to work the ranges. After that, beef cattle were raised on all Islands well into the 1970s, when the economics of shipping feed grain to the Islands made it prohibitive to raise animals to maturity here.

While most of today's ranchers ship out their stock as calves for raising on the mainland, there are a handful of producers committed to producing beef in the Islands for local consumption. These ranchers raise their beef without growth hormones and allow them to forage naturally on grasses and legumes in green pastures where they roam. Born, raised and processed here in the Islands, these cattle produce beef that is leaner than grain-fed, with a more robust, meaty flavor. Look for Island-raised beef and beef products like sausages at farmers markets and select food stores on each island.

Alex Franco, Kaupo Ranch Ltd.
Kaupo, Maui

Kaupo Ranch, established in 1927, is one of several beef cattle ranches on Maui that supplies premium beef under the Maui Cattle Company brand. Alex Franco has been with Kaupo Ranch since 1997. The biggest challenge facing farmers, says Franco, is how the state feels about agriculture. "It will take people who request and buy our product in the stores and restaurants, people who own agricultural land, people who own and operate businesses for our visitor industry to realize that the open spaces people enjoy won't be a part of the Hawai'i landscape in years to come if they don't purchase the product produced from it. Our islands are constantly changing, and if we want change to be headed in a positive direction, agriculture needs to be a big part of Hawai'i's economic equation, providing a sustainable future for the next generations."

Beef Stir Fry

Joan Namkoong, Freelance Food Writer

1   pound beef (flank, chuck or round)
3   tablespoons cornstarch
2   tablespoons soy sauce
2   tablespoons oil
6   cups Island-grown vegetables: asparagus, broccoli, or green or long beans
½   cup chicken broth
2   cloves minced garlic
2   teaspoons minced ginger
3   tablespoons oyster sauce
1   tablespoon mirin
2   tablespoons water
2   teaspoons sesame oil

Place beef in freezer for about 10 to 15 minutes. Cut into thin strips, about 1-inch x 2-inches. Place in a bowl, add 2 tablespoons cornstarch and soy sauce and mix well. Set aside.

Prepare vegetables: wash, drain well and cut into two-inch pieces.

Heat a wok or large skillet over high heat. Add oil and when it is hot, add the beef. Stir fry to brown the beef, just for a minute or two. Remove from pan. Add vegetables and broth and cook, covered for about two minutes. Uncover, add garlic, ginger, oyster sauce and mirin. Cook for two minutes then add beef and cook together for another minute. Mix remaining 1 tablespoon cornstarch and water and add to wok. Cook for 30 seconds then drizzle on sesame oil. Remove from heat and serve immediately.

Serves 4.

Meat Loaf
Joan Namkoong, Freelance Food Writer

1   pound Hawai'i-grown ground beef
¾   cup dry breadcrumbs
½   cup chicken broth or milk
½   cup finely chopped onion
1   egg
6   tablespoons ketchup
¼   cup chopped parsley
2   teaspoons salt
1   teaspoon pepper

Preheat oven to 350°F.

In a large bowl, soak breadcrumbs in broth or milk. Add beef and remaining ingredients and mix well. Place in a loaf pan and bake for about an hour. Slice to serve.

Serves 6.

BEETS

When buying, select firm and smooth beets, less than three inches in diameter, with crisp, bright greens. Cut greens one inch above the beet to prevent moisture loss. This also prevents loss of nutrients and color when cooking. Refrigerate in a plastic bag for up to two weeks.

To prepare beets, first scrub and clean them. Grate, slice or julienne beets to use as a colorful, crunchy raw garnish.

To boil, keep skins intact and taproot attached to help prevent staining during cooking. Boil whole in as little liquid and with as little heat as possible to retain their gorgeous color and sugar content. Lemon juice added while cooking brightens the color. Add salt at the end only.

To roast beets, rub skin with oil to prevent excess drying and scorching. Pierce then roast whole in their skins to achieve the perfect sugar concentration.

For fried beet chips, thinly slice and fry in oil at a temperature no higher than 275° F. Remove from oil, drain and fluff by tossing them around on a paper towel.

Beets provide you with fiber (nearly three grams per cooked cup) and magnesium (16% of daily value). Scientists believe the principle pigment in beets, beta-cyanin, may prevent chromosome damage, which is a first step on the road to cancer. Half a cup of cooked beets equals four or more daily servings of vegetables.

Roasted Beet and Goat Cheese Salad with Macadamias
Carol Nardello, Sub Zero/Wolf

3   medium red beets, trimmed, scrubbed, unpeeled
4   medium golden beets, trimmed, scrubbed, unpeeled
1   tablespoon olive oil
4½ ounces baby salad greens
½   cup macadamia nuts, chopped & toasted
5   ounces goat cheese, coarsely crumbled
3   tablespoons olive oil
2   tablespoons white balsamic vinegar
2   tablespoons orange juice
1½ teaspoons orange zest, grated
    Thin strips of orange peel

Preheat oven to 425° F.

Place beets in a baking pan and toss with 1 tablespoon oil. Seal tightly with aluminum foil and roast until tender, about one hour. Remove from oven, cool and peel. Cut into bite-size pieces.

Divide greens among six plates. Arrange beets on plates; top with nuts and goat cheese.

Whisk olive oil, vinegar, orange juice and zest. Drizzle over salads, garnish with strips of orange peel and serve.

Serves 6.

Roasted Beets with Maple Glaze
Carol Nardello, Sub Zero/Wolf

6   medium beets, trimmed and scrubbed
1   tablespoon olive oil
¼   cup butter
1   tablespoon cider vinegar
¼   cup maple syrup
    Salt and pepper to taste

Preheat oven to 425° F.

Place beets in a baking pan and toss with oil. Tightly seal with aluminum foil and bake until tender, about an hour and a quarter. When beets are cooked, slip off skins and slice into wedges.

Prepare glaze by melting butter in a saucepan. Add vinegar and syrup and simmer to reduce to about a quarter of a cup.

Add beets to glaze and season with salt and pepper. Place in heatproof serving bowl and return to warm oven to heat through.

Serves 4.

BREADFRUIT

B readfruit, or '*ulu* in Hawaiian, is a member of the fig family. This handsome evergreen tree originated in the South Pacific and is now found throughout the tropics. All Hawaiian islands have wild breadfruit trees; it is generally not a cultivated crop in Hawai'i. The luxurious leaves are large, glossy and dark-green, and fruits are usually round, oval, or elongated and weigh up to 10 pounds. The creamy white or pale yellow flesh, when roasted, is said to have the texture and fragrance of fresh-baked bread, giving the tree its name. Breadfruit is usually seedless, but many varieties do have seeds.

Breadfruit is the plant that the *H.M.S. Bounty* was carrying in the South Pacific when its crew mutinied. Captain Bligh's goal had been to transport the seedlings from Tahiti to the Caribbean, so that slaves there would have a ready source of starch and calories.

Buy breadfruit when the skin is light green, yellow-green, or yellow—unless it's the unusual variety with pinkish or orange-brown fruit. The thin skin is patterned with hexagonal markings and can be smooth, bumpy or spiny.

Refrigerate immediately, as breadfruit is highly perishable. It will last for up to two weeks in your refrigerator, depending upon freshness. To freeze, peel, cut into chunks and bag. It will keep for up to three months in the freezer.

Breadfruit is delicious as a replacement for potatoes. It can be used in soups or casseroles and is also delicious when peeled, sliced, and sautéed in butter.

'Ulu "Crackers"
Joan Namkoong, Freelance Food Writer

Serve these 'ulu "crackers" with a dip of mayonnaise and ketchup. They would also be terrific as a cracker base for smoked salmon or gravlax, caviar, crab dip or anything else you can think of.

1   breadfruit
     Oil for frying
     Sea salt or kosher salt

Peel breadfruit and remove core. Cut breadfruit into chunks, about 1½ to 2 inches.

Heat oil in a saucepan or deep fryer over medium high heat. When oil is hot, add breadfruit chunks in batches and cook until soft inside (test with a fork). Remove from the oil and drain. Keep oil hot.

With a flat-bottomed bowl or cup, flatten each breadfruit chunk. Return flattened pieces to the oil and fry until golden brown and crisp, about one to two minutes. Remove from the oil, drain on paper towels and sprinkle immediately with salt. Serve hot.

Serves 8-10.

'Ulu and Corn Chowder
Lori Wong, Culinary Consultant

7   strips bacon, chopped
1   large sweet onion, chopped
4   cups baked breadfruit, peeled and diced
2   cups water
2   cups fresh corn kernels, about 4-5 ears of corn
4   cups milk
1½ teaspoon Hawaiian salt
1   teaspoon ground pepper

In a large saucepan over medium heat, fry the bacon until almost crisp. Add the onion and cook until translucent. Add the breadfruit.

Add the water and simmer for five minutes, softening the breadfruit. Add corn, milk and seasonings. Bring to a boil, then lower the heat and simmer for 20 minutes. Serve hot.

Serves 4.

BROCCOLI

Broccoli, a member of the cabbage family, means "little sprouts" in Italian. Broccoli is a cool weather crop and the best-quality broccoli is produced in fall, late winter, and early spring. When the weather is too warm, broccoli heads become tough and fibrous. In Hawaiʻi, broccoli enjoys the cool weather climates of upcountry Maui and Kamuela on the Big Island.

Look for dark green broccoli, with tightly closed florets; avoid limp and yellowing bunches, or stems that appear cracked or dry. Color is also a nutrition indicator: florets that are dark green or purplish- or bluish-green have more beta-carotene and vitamin C than paler florets.

Broccoli needs to be trimmed and peeled before cooking. Remove the leaves and peel off the tough outer layer of the stem with a vegetable peeler or paring knife. Cut florets where they join the main stem. If florets are large, cut into smaller pieces. If blanching for crudités or stir-fry, avoid refreshing in cold water to retain maximum texture and flavor. While refreshing helps broccoli retain a vibrant color, texture and flavor are greatly compromised.

Broccoli raab, rabe or rapini resembles broccoli; they are both in the Brassica family, which also includes turnips. This slightly bitter, peppery vegetable is frequently used in Southern Italian cooking and is most commonly served steamed or sautéed with olive oil.

For broccoli raab, select vibrant crisp green bunches with tight flower heads and few bud clusters. Avoid yellowing flowers and stalks. Thinner stalks tend to be stringier than fatter ones.

Broccoli raab is grown in sandy soil, making a thorough washing important. Trim off the tough bottom stems, usually about ⅓ from the bottom. Many chefs prefer to blanch broccoli raab prior to sautéing to soften the bitter flavor of the greens.

Broccoli raab is best stored in an open plastic bag for up to four days in the coldest part of the refrigerator. Do not wash prior to storing, as water promotes deterioration. Storage in the refrigerator slows the conversion of sugar to lignin, thereby maintaining flavor and texture.

One cup of cooked broccoli has just 44 calories and is rich in calcium and the antioxidant vitamins C and E. Broccoli raab has 22 calories per 3½ ounce serving and is high in folic acid, potassium and vitamins A, C, and K.

Very Easy Broccoli Sauté
Melanie Kosaka, First Daughter Mediaworks

3   cups broccoli florets
¼   cup olive oil divided
1   tablespoon garlic, minced
     Red pepper flakes, to taste
     Salt and pepper

Use this broccoli sauté as a pizza topping, serve it over warm naan bread with a light cheese spread, black olives and sun-dried tomatoes, or combine it with pasta and cheese. You don't have to blanch the broccoli, making this a very quick and easy recipe.

In a 12-inch sauté pan heat about two tablespoons of olive oil and sauté the broccoli. Once the oil is absorbed and the broccoli begins to turn a bright green, add about an eighth of a cup of water to the pan to steam the broccoli. You may need to add more water if the broccoli needs to steam longer. This process should take about one minute. Once all the water is evaporated, make an opening in the broccoli in the middle of the sauté pan and add the remaining olive oil. Heat slightly, add garlic and sauté. Be sure not to brown the garlic, or it will add a bitter flavor to the dish. Season generously with salt, and add pepper and red pepper flakes to taste.

Serves 4.

Sautéed Broccoli Raab with Pancetta

Melanie Kosaka, First Daughter Mediaworks

Bitter broccoli raab is ideally paired with savory pancetta (Italian unsmoked bacon) in this quick sauté. Mix it with pasta for a one dish meal. Brush sliced baguette with olive oil and pan grill, spread with goat cheese and top with sautéed broccoli raab and pancetta and garnishes.

1	pound broccoli raab, trimmed
⅛	to ¼ cup olive oil
1	tablespoon fresh lemon juice
¾	pound pancetta, cut in medium dice
	Salt and pepper

GARNISH

Balsamic vinegar

Extra-virgin olive oil

Parmigiano-Reggiano

Blanch broccoli raab in a large pot of boiling water for about one minute. Drain and pat dry.

Heat a 12-inch skillet over medium heat and add olive oil. Sauté broccoli raab until tender, about three to four minutes. Drizzle lemon juice over broccoli raab and season with salt and pepper. Set aside on a serving platter. In the same sauté pan over medium heat cook the pancetta until tender; you may need to add several tablespoons of olive oil to keep it moist. Pour pancetta over broccoli raab. Garnish with a generous drizzle of extra-virgin olive oil and light drizzle of balsamic vinegar and top with shaved Parmigiano-Reggiano.

Serves 4.

CABBAGE

When we think of cabbage we think of the spherical light green firm heads of cabbage used in coleslaw or soups. But there are many more members of this family of Brassicas: won bok, bok choy, choy sum, mustard greens, kale, collards, broccoli, cauliflower, kohlrabi, Brussels sprouts. Most of these are grown in the Islands.

Cabbage and won bok (also known as Napa, celery or Chinese cabbage) can be eaten raw or cooked; other members of the family are usually cooked, steamed or stir-fried for best results.

When buying head cabbage, look for fresh firm heads that are heavy and solid. Store in a plastic bag in the vegetable crisper of your refrigerator. Cabbage will keep for up to two weeks, but its nutritive value will decrease with time.

To prepare cabbage, peel off outer leaves if wilted or yellowed. Cut head in half or in quarters, remove the hard core and cut into desired size. If you need whole leaves for stuffing or wrapping, remove the core from the bottom and plunge the whole cabbage in boiling water for 30 seconds and then into a bowl of ice water. Carefully remove the outer leaves, repeating the process as leaves become difficult to remove.

To prepare won bok, trim the bottom. Cut heads in half lengthwise and slice into desired size. Won bok has a milder flavor than head cabbage and a higher water content. It can be added to soups or Asian-style stews and cooks quickly. It is an ideal salad green: it is crunchy and does not wilt as quickly as delicate lettuces when dressed.

Chinese greens – bok choy, choy sum, Shanghai bok choy and tat soi – are tasty and versatile, especially in soups, appetizers and main dishes. With green or pearly white stalks and green leaves, these greens have mild, almost sweet stalks and cabbage-flavored leaves. Chinese greens can be used interchangeably.

When buying Chinese greens, look for thick stalks that are firm and crisp. Leaves should be crisp and green and have a fresh look about them. Store them in a perforated plastic bag in refrigerator crisper but use them within a day or two, as they will wilt. To prepare, trim off the base, discard blemished or tough leaves and wash well. Slice or chop and use in soups or stir-fry in a hot pan with a little oil, garlic and salt.

Collards, kale, Swiss chard and mustard greens are dark leafy greens that can be tough and fibrous are should be cooked. These greens have a stronger flavor and are sometimes bitter, but all are good sources of vitamins A and C, potassium, iron and calcium.

When buying these greens look for fresh, crisp leaves with firm, unblemished stems. More mature greens will be tougher and more strongly flavored. Remember that these greens contain mostly water, so they will shrink considerably when you cook them. What looks like a large bunch may only feed two people. Store in a plastic bag in the refrigerator for up to five days.

To prepare these greens, remove their stems and cut them to desired size. Cut leaves into pieces. Rinse well just before cooking. Cook stems first, as they will take longer, then cook leaves. Mustard greens, chard and kale marry well with bacon and onions; collards have an affinity for pork or ham hocks. Use kale in hearty soups, too.

Cabbage, Sausage and Garbanzo Bean Soup
Noreen Lam

4   cups cabbage, cut into 1-inch pieces
2   (4-5 ounces each) Portuguese sausages, cut into large dice
1   tablespoon olive oil
1   medium onion, cut into medium dice
2   stalks celery, cut into medium dice
1   (14½-ounce) can whole tomatoes, roughly chopped, include juice
1   (15-ounce) can garbanzo beans, drained
1   (14½-ounce) can low-sodium chicken stock
1   cup water
1   teaspoon fresh oregano
    Salt and pepper

In a large saucepan, sauté sausage in oil until lightly browned. Remove with a slotted spoon and set aside.

Add onions and celery to pan and cook until softened, about three minutes. Add the tomatoes, beans, stock, water, and oregano. Cover and simmer until vegetables are cooked, about 15 minutes.

Add cabbage and sausage; simmer a few additional minutes until cabbage is just cooked.

Adjust seasoning and serve.

Serves 6.

Cabbage and Sweet Potato Gratin
Noreen Lam

½   head cabbage, roughly chopped, about 8 cups
2   medium sweet potatoes
1   cup Gruyère or Jarlsberg cheese, grated
4   tablespoons unsalted butter
3   tablespoons flour
2   cups milk, or 1 cup milk and 1 cup chicken stock
½   cup Parmesan, grated
    Salt and pepper
    Nutmeg
    Butter for topping

Preheat oven to 375° F.

Blanch the cabbage in lightly salted water 10-15 seconds and drain well in a large colander. When cool enough to handle, squeeze out excess water.

Cook the sweet potatoes in lightly salted water, until just done but still firm. Drain and cool. Peel and cut into slices. Layer on the bottom of a buttered 9-inch x 9-inch glass or ceramic baking dish. Lightly salt and pepper the potatoes and sprinkle with half of the cheese. Layer cabbage over cheese.

Make the white sauce by melting the butter in a saucepan over medium heat. Whisk in the flour to make a roux and continue to cook it about two minutes, stirring constantly. Slowly add the milk and/or stock. Continue to stir until the sauce comes up to a boil, reduce the heat and simmer for 15 minutes until thick, stirring occasionally. Season generously with salt, pepper and nutmeg.

Pour the sauce over the cabbage, spreading it evenly over the top. Sprinkle the remaining cheese over the top, followed by the Parmesan. Dot with additional butter if desired.

Bake for 40-45 minutes until bubbling and brown on the top. Let rest a few minutes before serving.

Serves 6 as a side dish.

Dean's Tsukemono
Dean Okimoto, Nalo Farms

5-6   pounds mustard greens and daikon
2   tablespoons Hawaiian salt
1½   tablespoons dashi-no-mono*
½   cup water
3   tablespoons fresh grated ginger and juice
½   cup fresh lime juice
½   cup soy sauce
       Chili pepper water (optional to taste)

Coarsely chop the mustard greens and daikon and place in large glass or ceramic bowl. Toss with the salt. Place a plate or board on top – make sure it fits inside the bowl, so it rests directly on the vegetables – and weight it with bricks, cans, or jars. Let stand for six to eight hours.

Drain the vegetables and squeeze the cabbage by handfuls to remove as much water as possible. Combine the rest of the ingredients and pour the mixture over the greens and daikon. Let stand at least four hours before serving.

Serves a crowd.

*Dashi-no-mono is an instant Japanese soup stock made from dried kelp (dashi konbu) and dried bonito (katsuo-bushi) and comes in a jar or packet in granular form. It can be found in the Asian food section of most markets.

Dumplings with Won Bok, Tofu and Shiitake Mushrooms
Noreen Lam

4   cups won bok (½ medium head)
½   block (7 ounces) firm tofu
1   tablespoon vegetable oil
1-2 cloves garlic, minced
1   tablespoon fresh ginger, minced
2   cups fresh shiitake mushrooms, diced
½   cup green onions, cut into thin rounds
1   tablespoon sesame seeds
1   tablespoon miso
2   teaspoons soy sauce
1   package won ton or gyoza wrappers
½   teaspoon salt, or to taste
     Pinch pepper

Drain and weight tofu for several hours or overnight.

Cut the won bok leaves in half lengthwise and then across into fine strips. Place in a colander and sprinkle with a little salt. Toss and let stand about an hour. By handfuls, squeeze out excess moisture and put the won bok in a bowl.

Heat the oil in a frying pan and add the garlic, ginger and mushrooms. Cook until the mushrooms are tender, about three minutes. Cool.

Crumble the drained tofu into the won bok, and add the mushrooms and the rest of the ingredients. Mix until combined, adjusting salt if necessary. Form dumplings using a tablespoon of filling for each, sealing the edges well with a little water.

Cook in boiling salted water for five to six minutes until the wrappers are cooked. Drain and serve with your favorite dipping sauce or in broth.

Makes about 24 dumplings.

Kamuela Chinese Cabbage Salad with Won Ton Chips
Kamuela Farmers

1   head won bok, sliced thin
⅓   cup mayonnaise
½   cup white vinegar
½   cup sugar
1   cup vegetable oil
1   clove garlic, minced
½   teaspoon black pepper
2   teaspoons salt
1   teaspoon dry mustard
     Won ton chips

Combine dressing ingredients and shake well. Chill before serving. Serve over thin slices of won bok. Top with won ton chips.
        Serves 6.

Asian Slaw
Noreen Lam

4   cups won bok, cut into ¼-inch strips
1   cup red cabbage, finely shredded
1   cup bean sprouts
1   medium carrot, peeled and cut into fine julienne
2   stalks celery, cut into thin diagonal strips
½   red bell pepper, cut into thin strips
2   stalks green onion, cut thin on the diagonal
    Roasted peanuts, chopped or sesame seed for garnish

DRESSING
2   tablespoons fish sauce
2   tablespoons rice wine vinegar
2   tablespoons fresh lemon juice
1   tablespoon sugar
1   tablespoon sweet chili sauce

Soak the red cabbage and pepper in cold water for a few minutes to prevent them from bleeding into the salad. Drain and dry well. Combine all the vegetables in a bowl.

Combine dressing ingredients in a small bowl and stir until sugar is dissolved. Toss vegetables with the dressing just before serving. Garnish with the peanuts or sesame seeds.

Serves 4.

Chinese Greens, Tofu, and Shiitake Mushrooms
Kay Tokunaga, Contemporary Museum Café

½   pound bok choy or choy sum
1   tablespoon vegetable oil
2   cloves garlic, minced
6   shiitake mushrooms, stemmed and sliced
½   block firm tofu, cubed
2   cups water
2   tablespoons soy sauce
1   tablespoon oyster sauce
¼   cup water plus 1 tablespoon cornstarch

Heat oil over medium heat in a medium skillet. Add garlic and sauté one to two minutes. Add mushrooms and a little water. Cook until mushrooms are soft. Add greens. Lay tofu on top of bok choy. Add water, soy, and oyster sauce. Simmer until bok choy is tender. Add cornstarch mixture and bring to a boil to thicken. Adjust seasoning.

Serve on chow mein noodles or over steamed rice or as a side dish.

Grelos
Wanda Adams, Food Editor, *The Honolulu Advertiser*

1   bunch collard greens or kale, finely shredded
1-3 cloves garlic, minced
½   sweet onion, minced
     Extra-virgin olive oil
     Salt and pepper
     Water or stock

In the late nineteenth and early twentieth century, every Portuguese-Hawaiian home with a strip of soil alongside it had three things planted thereon: flat-leaf parsley; tiny, hot chili peppers and as many Portuguese cabbage plants as they could make room for—the beloved couves (koo-vzh).

Larousse Gastronomique lists cabbage or couves as one of the four dominant ingredients of Portuguese cooking. Portuguese cabbage is an upright, large, leafy, loose-headed light-to-bright green vegetable for which collard greens or kale can be used interchangeably.

Couves are almost always cut into strips or shredded. Wash greens well, trim or cut away tough central rib and stems. Lay the leaves one on top of the other, roll into a cigar and trim crossways, very, very thinly.

The simplest preparation for greens in the Portuguese tradition is grelos—sautéed cabbage. This is best with the youngest, most tender greens; add bits of rendered bacon or salt pork for more flavor.

Heat a large, heavy-bottomed sauté pan over medium-high heat. Add a good splash of olive oil and heat. Add the minced garlic and onions to the hot oil, turn down the heat to medium and cook until they are limp and beginning to change color.

Add the shredded greens and sauté until bright green but cooked through, a few minutes, adding a tablespoon or two of water or stock as needed to help them cook.

Remove from the heat, add salt and pepper to taste and serve as a side dish. Portuguese like a splash of vinegar with this; a squeeze of lemon is also lovely (but it will turn the greens grayish).

Serves 4.

Pizza with Swiss Chard, Feta, Olives and Red Onions
Kay Tokunaga, Contemporary Museum Café

½   pound Swiss chard, trimmed
4   Pita
    Kalamata olives, diced
    Red onion, thin slivers
    Feta cheese, crumbled

Blanch Swiss chard in salted water, drain, squeeze and chop. Brush pita with olive oil. Top with chard, olives, onions, and cheese. Bake for 15 minutes at 350° F.
Serves 4.

Larry Jefts, Jefts Farms
Kunia, Oʻahu

Every week Jefts Farms, a group of interrelated businesses and brand names, produces a pound of food for every man, woman and child living in the Islands. "We are ubiquitous," says owner Larry Jefts, a farmer for 49 years, 28 of them here in Hawaiʻi. He means that the products his farms grow are the products Islanders use every day: cabbage, tomatoes, bananas, bell peppers and other kitchen staples. He also means they market at almost every level of the chain – grocery stores, swap meets, Chinatown stalls, cruise ships, military messes.

Jefts says he likes the integrity of farming. "It's a good, honest business where you're feeding people. . .a necessary profession." He uses the word "profession" advisedly: "It's not a lifestyle; it's not open space and all of that. It's a profession and the reward is feeding people."

Jefts says the future of agriculture in the Islands is in the hands of the people: "The 1.2 million people in Hawaiʻi have an opportunity, if they take it, to transition some of this agricultural land into a bread basket for themselves. We've been very successful industrially, raising pineapple and sending sugar around the world, but what we could do with this property here now is put things on our table." Not all the land zoned agricultural is viable for food production, he says, but if we're wise enough to reserve the percentage that is, we'll reap the reward.

Kolors of Maui Sunset Slaw

Warren Watanabe, President, Maui County Farm Bureau

This recipe showcases the colorful array of vegetables grown in Upcountry Maui. If you can't find the various colors of cauliflower, use a combination of cauliflower and broccoli or other fresh locally grown vegetables.

2   cups thinly sliced green cabbage
2   cups green cauliflower florets
1   cup purple cauliflower florets
½   cup orange cauliflower florets
½   cup thinly sliced pink and yellow chard leaves
½   cup thinly sliced red chard stems
½   small Kula onion, thinly sliced

DRESSING
⅓   cup apple cider vinegar
½   teaspoon salt
⅓   teaspoon celery seed
3   tablespoons vegetable oil
2-3 tablespoons frozen apple juice concentrate
     Juice of half a lemon
     Fresh ground black pepper to taste

Place cabbage in the bottom of a salad bowl. Place remaining vegetables in bowl, arranging in a decorative pattern to show off the colors.

In a small bowl whisk together dressing ingredients until well blended. Pour over vegetables and serve at once.

Serves 6.

CHOCOLATE

C acao trees only grow in a narrow band 20 degrees north or south of the equator, making Hawai'i the only place in the United States that can support commercial cacao production. Locally produced chocolate has been around for less than 20 years, but with the great growing conditions in Hawai'i, the new Hawaiian chocolate industry has a great head start.

Cacao trees produces fewer than 100 pods per year. (Cacao is known as cocoa only when it is harvested.) The pods are extremely colorful when ripe, ranging from red and purple to yellow, orange and even magenta.

Pods contain large white "beans" that must be fermented before being processed. Farmers ferment the beans in wooden boxes for about one week, then dry them in the sun for about a month. Once dry, the pods are carefully roasted, then hulled to release the meat of the nut (called the "nib"). The nibs are put through a process called "conching," in which they are put into a spinning refiner that grinds and presses them together with sugar, vanilla, lecithin and other ingredients that merge into a chocolate paste called "liquor" (it's non-alcoholic!). The processing gives the chocolate a smooth texture and removes some of the bitterness.

Unsweetened chocolate is pure chocolate liquor that has been cooled and formed into bars. Also known as bitter chocolate, it is best for recipes that can stand a really solid dose of chocolaty flavor. Cocoa powder contains only 10 to 24 percent cocoa butter, which is where the fat in choco-late comes from, so it can add some nice chocolate flavor to your treats without adding as many calories. So-called white chocolate is actually not a chocolate since it doesn't contain any cocoa solids, but it must be at least 20 percent pure cocoa butter. Milk chocolate is the type of chocolate most commonly used in candy bars and commercial chocolate snacks. Milk chocolate must contain at least 10 percent chocolate liquor and 12 percent milk solids. Very smooth, sweet and easy on the palate, it's great for snack-ing, but not so great for baking.

Bittersweet (dark or semi-sweet) chocolate contains anywhere from 35 to 75 percent chocolate liquor. Strong in chocolate flavors and with a smooth texture, this type is most commonly used for mixing into chocolate desserts. The intensity varies with the percentage of liquor, sugar, as well as the manufacturer and the care taken in the manufacturing process.

Dark chocolate is considered one of the "super foods," a short list of foods high in nutrients and antioxidants. Chocolate also contains natural stimulants that increase your alertness and fight fatigue. Even better, eating chocolate can raise the level of your HDL, or "good," cholesterol. But 55 to 65 percent of chocolate's calories come from fat. The average American eats more than 12 pounds of chocolate a year. For the greatest benefit, enjoy your chocolate for its nutrients and delicious taste, but go for quality, not quantity.

More Chocolate Morsels

The melting point for cocoa butter is about the same as our body tem-perature, which is why it melts so smoothly and pleasantly on the tongue.

Never refrigerate or freeze chocolate. The cocoa butter in your choco-late will easily absorb flavors from other foods. Simply wrap your chocolate tightly in plastic and store in a cool, dry place. Properly stored, milk and white chocolates will maintain their flavors for six months to a year. Dark chocolate can actually last several years with care – if you don't eat it up long before that!

Chocolate Sauce
Abigail Langlas, Honolulu Coffee Company

A rich chocolaty sauce to drizzle over ice cream or anything you fancy.

2½ cups bittersweet chocolate
1   cup heavy cream
½   cup sugar
½   cup water

Boil cream, sugar, and water together and pour over chocolate; stir until smooth. Keep in a covered container in the refrigerator.
Makes about 4 cups.

Chocolate Decadence
Abigail Langlas, Honolulu Coffee Company

Deep chocolate flavor will satisfy any chocoholic's craving in this flourless cake.

3   cups semi-sweet chocolate
6   ounces unsalted butter
¾   cup macadamia nut oil
6   eggs
½   cup granulated sugar
¼   cup Grand Marnier liqueur

Preheat oven to 300° F. Grease an 8-inch springform pan and line with parchment or wax paper, or use a dozen greased half-cup-size cupcake cups.

In a saucepan melt chocolate, butter and oil. Remove from heat and cool.

Whip eggs and sugar about 10 minutes until thick and creamy. Add Grand Marnier and blend. Fold chocolate mixture into egg mixture.

Pour mixture into pan and bake for 25 minutes, or 12 minutes for individual cakes. Remove from oven and cool completely. Refrigerate for several hours before removing from pan.

Serves 12.

Warm Chocolate Cake
Abigail Langlas, Honolulu Coffee Company

A light soufflé-like cake encases a sauce-like interior that runs as you cut into it – simply delicious.

1   cup bittersweet chocolate
6   ounces unsweetened butter
5   eggs
1   cup granulated sugar
½   cup flour
3   tablespoons dark rum
2   teaspoons vanilla

Pre-heat the oven to 350° F. Coat 10 ceramic ramekins with butter and lightly dust with flour and set aside.

In the top of a double boiler, melt chocolate and butter. Cool.

In a large bowl, beat eggs and sugar until sugar is dissolved. Add chocolate mixture to egg mixture. Sift flour over the chocolate mixture and combine to make a smooth mixture. Add rum and vanilla and blend well. Divide among ramekins and bake for 12 minutes. The center of the cake should still be soft and runny.

Serve in ramekins or, using a butter knife, loosen the edges of the cake and gently turn over onto a plate. To garnish, dust lightly with powdered sugar, raspberries and a good-quality vanilla bean ice cream.

Serves 10.

Kona Coffee Mousse Cake on Dark Chocolate Macadamia Nut Cookie Crust Cathy Barrett, Kailua Candy Company

This recipe utilizes three very special Big Island-grown products: Original Hawaiian Chocolate Factory chocolate, Hawaiian Vanilla Company vanilla extract and Kona coffee. Look for these products at farmers markets or specialty shops.

CRUST

2 ⅔ ounces Original Hawaiian Chocolate Factory's dark chocolate, melted
⅔ cup dry-roasted macadamia nut chips
⅓ cup unsalted butter
¼ cup brown sugar
¼ cup sugar
1 egg
⅔ cup flour
½ teaspoon baking soda
¼ teaspoon salt
Splash of Hawaiian Vanilla Company vanilla extract

Preheat oven to 375° F.

In a mixing bowl, beat butter until creamy. Gradually add the two sugars and beat until light. Add the egg and beat well. Mix in the melted chocolate and vanilla. Stir the flour, baking soda and salt into the chocolate mixture until well blended. Fold in the macadamia nuts.

Line a 9-inch springform pan with parchment paper. Spread dough evenly in the bottom of the pan. Bake in oven for seven to nine minutes. Remove and cool.

Mᴏᴜssᴇ
1   pound Original Hawaiian Chocolate Factory's dark chocolate, melted.
⅔   cup 100% Kona Coffee Dark Roast coffee, brewed
2   egg whites
1   cup heavy cream

Place melted chocolate in a large bowl. Add the coffee and mix with a wire whisk until smooth.

Whip egg whites in mixer until soft peaks form. Fold into chocolate/coffee mixture. Whip the cream and fold into the chocolate/coffee/egg white mixture until well blended.

Spray sides of the pan with the cookie crust in the bottom with non-stick vegetable oil spray. Pour mousse on top of cooled cookie crust. Refrigerate until set (overnight). Remove cake from pan. Prepare ganache to pour over cake.

Gᴀɴᴀᴄʜᴇ
¼   cup heavy cream.
2   ounces Original Hawaiian Chocolate Factory's dark chocolate, melted

In a microwave-safe bowl, heat cream in microwave until hot (one minute). Pour on top of melted chocolate and stir gently with wire whisk until smooth. Immediately pour over mousse cake and refrigerate until serving.

Serves 8-10.

Citrus

Citrus fruits are especially sweet in Hawai'i, where the warm sun enhances the sugars in the fruit. Pomelo (also known as jabong), grapefruit, oranges, tangerines, lemons, limes, calamondin and kumquats all fare well in many an Island backyard. But there are few commercial farmers of citrus fruit, so farmers markets are the ideal place to find these juicy, tasty offerings.

The most popular commercially farmed citrus is the mottled "Hawaiian orange," also known as the Kona Gold or Ka'u orange. These come mostly from the southern part of the Big Island. Don't be turned off by their yellow-green-brown skin; inside, the orangey-yellow sections burst forth with lots of juice and sugar. Eat them out of hand or squeeze for the best orange juice ever.

Winter is cold and flu season, but fortunately, it is also the best time to find cold-fighting citrus fruits. So peel and indulge in pomelos, tangerines and sweet local oranges for the Vitamin C, cholesterol-blocking pectin and folate, plus the additional benefits of soluable and nonsoluble fiber.

Eating fresh citrus fruit out of hand is the best and most delicious way to enjoy them. The more acidic Meyer lemons, Hawaiian lemons and Key limes are best juiced, but don't forget the zest, which adds a bright note to salads, cookies and cakes.

Hawaiian lemons are juicy specimens and usually much larger than their Sunkist counterparts. What to do when you have lots of lemons? Make lemonade, of course.

Great Lemonade
Sharon Kobayashi and Ruth Arakaki, Latitude 22

Refreshing and light, this lemonade is simply wonderful. You can easily double or triple the recipe and adjust to your taste.

1   cup fresh-squeezed Meyer or Hawaiian lemon juice
     (about 5 large lemons' worth)
1   cup candied mint syrup
     Water (4-5 cups plus ice) to taste
     Club soda to taste

CANDIED MINT SYRUP
1   bunch of mint
1½   cups sugar
1   cups water

Bring syrup ingredients to a boil; cook for one minute. Cool thoroughly. Pour one cup of cooled syrup (and leaves) into a blender and blend until leaves are well minced. Strain out any large pieces of mint leaves. You can store the candied mint syrup in the refrigerator for several weeks.

Add lemon juice and water to mint syrup, mix well. Chill. Before serving, add club soda to taste.

Tips: you can mix the lemon juice and mint syrup to use as a base for easier storage in the refrigerator. Add the water directly to the punch bowl. You can also store this base in the freezer for up to three months.

Replace some of the water with vodka or light rum, and you have a cocktail that would do Hemingway proud. Replace the club soda with more water and heat in the microwave for a relaxing and cold-busting nightcap.

Grilled Citrus Mojo
Sharon Kobayashi and Ruth Arakaki, Latitude 22

Based on a Columbian herb salsa, this tangy mojo enlivens roasted Kabocha squash and grilled meats and seafood, and can be used as a light dressing for salads, especially a selection of orange slices, fresh hearts of palm and avocado. Grilling or broiling the citrus mellows the fruit, as well as making it much easier to juice. It is best to use the mojo within two or three days.

4   tangerines or tangelos
4   Meyer or Hawaiian lemons or large limes
½   cup extra-virgin olive oil (plus extra for baking)
12   cloves garlic, minced
3   tablespoons cumin seed, ground
1   tablespoon coriander seed, ground
1   cup cilantro, chopped
1   cup Italian parsley, chopped
4   jalapenos, seeded and minced

Preheat grill or broiler on high.

Collect 1 teaspoon zest from tangerines and 1 teaspoon zest from lemons. Reserve. Cut citrus fruits in half, brush cut side with olive oil. Arrange on broiler pan; trim bottoms of fruit so they will sit flat. With cut side facing the heat source, grill or broil fruit until golden brown.

Remove fruit from heat, cool completely, juice and strain seeds and pulp. Combine juice, zest and other ingredients. Season with salt and pepper. Let mojo rest, covered, in refrigerator for one to two hours to allow flavors to mingle.

Season mojo with salt and pepper and use 1½ cups mojo to cook with a whole chicken (four to six pounds) or steak, pork, or shrimp (two to four pounds). Spoon the remaining mojo over the cooked meat or seafood before serving.

Makes two and a half or three cups of sauce.

COCONUT

C oconuts are available all year throughout the state. To open a husked coconut, try either of these methods:

1. Make an imaginary line around the middle of a coconut (between the two ends) and using a hammer, tap around the line until you come back to where you started. The coconut should split open. You may need to give the coconut an extra tap. Break open over a bowl to catch the water.

2. Puncture two of the soft "eyes" with an ice pick and drain out the water. Put the coconut in a shallow pan in a 300° F oven for 45 minutes. If the coconut doesn't crack, tap it with a hammer – it should split.

To remove coconut meat from shell; use a paring knife. Peel the brown skin. Shells can be used as serving bowls. Grate coconut using a coconut grater, box grater or food processor. Fresh coconut meat will keep three to four days in refrigerator and will freeze nicely.

Coconut Milk
Holly Hadsell-El Hajji, Orchid's Sky Catering

2   cups grated coconut
1   cup boiling water

Place coconut in a bowl and pour boiling water over coconut. Let stand for 20-25 minutes. Strain through double thickness cheesecloth, pressing to remove all the liquid.
Makes 1 cup.

Coconut Margarita
Holly Hadsell-El Hajji, Orchid's Sky Catering

1   shot glass of coconut milk
1   shot tequila
     Juice of 1 lime
     Splash Cointreau

Shake ingredients together with ice and serve.

Poisson Cru
Holly Hadsell-El Hajji, Orchid's Sky Catering

2   pounds extremely fresh high-grade ahi, cut into 1-inch pieces
1   sweet onion, chopped in 1-inch pieces
1   green bell pepper, chopped in 1-inch pieces
1   cucumber, cut into rounds
2   tomatoes, cut into wedges
2   cups fresh coconut milk
     Juice of 3 limes
     Salt to taste

Mix all ingredients – the lime juice will "cook" the ahi – and serve on a bed of lettuce.

Serves 6-8 as an appetizer.

COFFEE

In 1813, Don Francisco de Paula y Marin, a Spaniard in Kamehameha I's court, was the first to plant coffee trees on Oʻahu. Brazilian trees of the *Arabica* variety were cultivated in Mānoa Valley in the 1920s, and cuttings were transported to Kona in 1828. Hawaiian coffee became a commercial crop in 1930 and has turned into a multi-million-dollar industry in the Islands. The only commercially grown coffee in the United States is grown in Hawaiʻi. Today coffee is grown on the islands of Hawaiʻi, Oʻahu, Maui, Molokaʻi and Kauaʻi.

Coffee originally comes from the east coast of Africa and the Arabian Peninsula. Coffee trees grow best at high altitudes with warm days and cool nights. It's said that the Kona area of the Big Island has a perfect environment for growing high-quality Arabica coffee.

The fruit of the coffee tree is called the "cherry," for the red color of the ripe fruit. Raw coffee *beans*, however, are actually dull green before they are roasted and take on their familiar brown tones, the shades of which help to predict the flavors of the final product. Roasting brings out and enhances the natural flavors locked inside the beans. Lightly roasted beans have a high acidity, but retain lighter, subtler notes. Dark roasts are richer in flavor, but can overpower the more delicate overtones of a bean.

Good coffee offers flavors nearly as varied as those of wine. The natural aromatic oils of the coffee bean easily spread across your palate, making coffee one of the most robust, mouth-filling flavors of any food. Chocolate, flowers, smoke, leather and mud are flavors tossed into discussions about a sip of coffee.

With coffee, the rule is always the fresher the better. To keep your coffee at its freshest and keep in those delicious (but volatile) oils, you need to keep your coffee sealed in an airtight, lightproof container and store it in a cool place. It should stay fresh for three to four days. It's not always a good idea to refrigerate or freeze coffee. The cold will dry out coffee beans, and the oils in ground coffee absorb odors very easily. Coffee beans will keep in the freezer for two to three weeks. Don't even think about it with ground coffee.

Ray Kunitake, Waiaha Farm
Hōlualoa, Hawai'i

A third-generation coffee farmer, Ray Kunitake was once a jeweler but decided to return to the family farm that has been producing fine Kona estate coffee since the 1920s. The 28-acre farm is at 1,200 feet elevation, ideal for growing this prized coffee.

The Kunitake family handpicks their coffee cherries during the December harvest season. They take pride in pulping their own beans and carefully selecting the beans that go into the end product. Ray loves to see lots of blossoms on the trees, an indication of a good season.

"I love being my own boss," says Ray about farming. "I also love nature and working with the land. I see things happen that most people don't get to experience."

Kona Coffee Crème Brulée
Abigail Langlas, Honolulu Coffee Company

⅓   cup crushed Kona coffee beans
1½   cups whipping cream
6   egg yolks
6   tablespoons granulated sugar

In a small saucepan, bring the cream and the crushed coffee beans to a simmer. Take the cream off the heat and let the coffee infuse for about 10 minutes.

Whisk the egg yolks and add the sugar. When the coffee cream is ready, strain onto the egg mixture, whisking continuously so as not to cook the egg yolks.

Pour the mixture into six deep ramekins or glass dishes and place them in a 9-inch x 13-inch baking pan filled with water up to half the height of the ramekins. Bake for about one hour at 250° F. Cream should be set, still soft, but not jiggly in the center.

Chill the crème brulée for a couple hours to set. Before serving, sprinkle with granulated or raw sugar and, using a butane torch, caramelize the top to create a golden brown sugar crust.

Serves 6.

Tips: Small baking torches can be easily found in many cooking stores these days, but if you do not have one, you can also put the brulées under the broiler for a few minutes to caramelize. Be careful not to burn. To crush coffee beans, use a rolling pin. Do not grind.

Kona Coffee Pannacotta

Abigail Langlas, Honolulu Coffee Company

1¼ cups very strong Kona coffee or espresso
5   (¼ ounce) packages powdered gelatin
1   cup water
1   (13½ ounce) can sweetened condensed milk
2   cups heavy cream

Spray 12 ramekins with a light coating of non-stick spray and set aside.

Sprinkle gelatin onto water and dissolve.

Heat sweetened condensed milk, cream and coffee together. Remove from heat and add gelatin to dissolve. Cool.

Pour mixture into prepared glass dishes. Refrigerate for a few hours to set. Unmold onto a plate or serve in glasses.

Serves 12.

CORN

S upersweet corn is one of Hawai'i's finest crops: crunchy sweet and so wonderful when it's eaten freshly picked. Ears of corn are ripe about 10 weeks after planting and best about 16 to 20 days after the silk forms. When you're buying fresh corn, look for darker-colored silk that's not mushy and black. Kernel color is not an indication of the corn's maturity or sweetness: different shades of yellow indicate the variety of the corn.

The crunch and sweetness of an ear are functions of how the corn is handled after harvest. The closer to picking that you eat the corn, the better the quality will be. Refrigeration is also important: ears of corn should be chilled as soon after picking as possible. So when you're buying corn at a farmers market, you should plan on keeping it cool on the ride home. It'll make a difference!

You will often find Hawai'i-grown corn lopped off at the top. This is done to remove a caterpillar that loves to feast on the sweet corn. To cut kernels off the ears, hold the ear vertically with a cut end on a cutting board. Using a sharp knife, slice off the kernels. Scrape the cob with the back of the knife to get juices or, if you're making chowder, boil the cobs in the liquid to get flavor and sweetness. Two to three ears of corn will yield about a cup of kernels.

If fresh corn is plentiful, blanch the ears for one to two minutes in boiling water; cool immediately in ice water. Freeze as kernels or as whole ears. You'll be glad you did when fresh corn is not readily available.

Succotash
College of Tropical Agriculture and Human Resources
University of Hawai'i at Mānoa

Adapted from "Supersweet Corn-Ucopia," a cook-booklet

1   cup corn kernels
1   cup soybeans (edamane), cooked
2   tablespoons butter
1   tablespoon onion, minced
1   cup cream
    Salt and pepper to taste

In a sauté pan, heat butter over medium high heat. Add corn, soybeans and onion and sauté for a few minutes. Add cream and simmer for about three minutes to reduce the liquid. Season to taste and serve hot. Serves 4-6.

Corn Relish

College of Tropical Agriculture and Human Resources
University of Hawai'i at Mānoa, Fruit and Vegetable Education Project

1   cup corn kernels
1   cup green onions, chopped
1   cup sweet red pepper, chopped
4   tablespoons vinegar
3   tablespoons sugar
½   teaspoon celery seed
    Salt and pepper to taste

Combine all ingredients in a saucepan and simmer over medium heat, covered for 5 minutes. Uncover and continue to cook until liquid evaporates. Remove from heat and cool; refrigerate and serve cold.
Serves 4.

Corn Custard

College of Tropical Agriculture and Human Resources
University of Hawai'i at Mānoa

Adapted from "Supersweet Corn-Ucopia," a cook-booklet

1   cup corn kernels, blanched
2   eggs
1   cup bread crumbs
1   cup milk
½   cup cream
2   tablespoons butter, melted
1   teaspoon sugar
     Salt

Preheat oven to 350° F.

Beat eggs until fluffy. Add other ingredients and blend well. Pour into a casserole and bake for 50 to 60 minutes or until set. Remove from oven, cool slightly and serve.

Serves 6.

EGGPLANT

In America, eggplant was once thought to be poisonous, but in India, the Middle East and Asia, where it is used the most, eggplant is prized for its soft but meaty texture and its capacity to soak up the flavors of spices and seasonings. Eggplant is actually a fruit, related to the potato and tomato, and there are many varieties of this member of the nightshade family.

You can choose from the large teardrop-shaped globes to small, rather bitter cherry-sized eggplant and long Japanese eggplant, each one well suited to a variety of preparations.

Choose eggplants that are firm and heavy for their size with shiny and unwrinkled skin. You can store them in the refrigerator for four days, though they will begin to wrinkle. When using large eggplant, it's a good idea to salt the pieces to draw out any bitterness; skinny Japanese eggplants don't require this. The bitterness of the small cherry-like eggplants, in contrast, is part of what makes their flavor prized in Thai cooking.

Caponata
Tish Uyehara, Armstrong Produce

Caponata is a classic Italian salad or relish that combines fresh eggplant with zesty tomatoes, capers, olives and pine nuts. In this version, use diced macadamia nuts for a little crunch.

4	long Japanese eggplant, cut into ½-inch thick half-moons
⅓	cup olive oil
1	sweet onion, sliced
3	cloves garlic, minced
2-3	tomatoes, diced
2	tablespoons capers
¼	cup pitted Kalamata olives
2-3	tablespoons red wine vinegar
½	cup fresh basil cut into julienne
¼	cup diced macadamia nuts
	Salt and freshly ground black pepper

In a large sauté pan over medium high heat, heat the olive oil. When it is hot, add the eggplant, onion and garlic and sauté until eggplant is soft and brown, about 10 to 15 minutes.

Add tomatoes, capers, olives and red wine vinegar. Cover, lower heat and simmer until eggplant and onion are tender, about 10 minutes, stirring occasionally. When the mixture is well cooked, season with salt and pepper. Add basil and toss together. Transfer to serving dish and sprinkle with macadamia nuts. Serve at room temperature or chilled; it may be made ahead and stored in the refrigerator for two days. Serve with toasted bread.

Serves 8 as an appetizer.

Grilled Eggplant
Matsuda-Fukuyama Farm/Kahuku Brand

3-4 Japanese eggplant
     Olive oil

SAUCE
1   cup soy sauce
½   cup water
1   tablespoon chili paste
¼   cup lime juice
1   tablespoon minced ginger

Heat a grill or broiler. Cut eggplant in half lengthwise. Brush gener-ously with olive oil and grill for two to three minutes on each side.

Blend sauce ingredients together. Cut eggplant into bite-sized pieces and dip in sauce to serve.

Serves 6-8 as an appetizer.

FENNEL

Fennel has a mild licorice flavor and a nice crunch. It can also be cooked in a variety of ways, but the cool anise flavor is a great accompaniment to any dish. For variations on fennel slaw or salad, add some orange juice or zest, orange sections or apple slices. Toss in watercress or arugula leaves. Add shaved parmesan and some fresh black pepper. Garnish with a little frond of fennel leaves.

Choose a fennel bulb that is large (less waste) and isn't too bruised or too fibrous looking. It should be a pale, almost white color. Reserve leaves for steaming with fish or for use in stocks. Wrap fennel in plastic and refrigerate.

To prepare, remove any stalks at the top of the bulb. Clean and wash the fennel bulb. Remove any bruises and trim a little of the root end. Quarter from top to bottom and remove some of the hard core, leaving enough to hold the fennel together for slicing.

Lemongrass Fennel Salad
Olelo pa'a Faith Ogawa, Dining by Faith

This refreshing salad is delicious with fresh poached salmon or smoked salmon.

4   small fennel bulbs, very thinly sliced
¼   cup lime juice
1   tablespoon fish sauce
2   tablespoons raw sugar
2   tablespoons lemongrass, minced

Combine lime juice, fish sauce, raw sugar and lemongrass in a bowl and mix. Place the thinly sliced fennel in the bowl and toss.
Serves 4.

Fresh Fennel Slaw
Cheryl To, PacifiKool

1   large bulb of fennel
3   tablespoons extra-virgin olive oil
2   tablespoons fresh lemon juice
    Kosher salt

Slice the fennel in thin long slices. Place in a bowl, drizzle with olive oil and lemon juice, and sprinkle with a little salt. Toss fennel until all ingredients are evenly dispersed. Taste and adjust flavorings. Cover and chill for approximately 15 minutes before serving to let flavors blend. The fennel should be slightly crisp.
Serves 4.

GREEN BEANS

Green beans can be yellow, purple, white or green, and they can be flat or round. Bright in color, crisp in texture and full of vegetable-y flavor, green beans are simply delicious steamed, stirfried or served chilled in a salad. Nuts marry well with green beans; butter, dill, lemon and orange do, too. When shopping, look for beans that have a smooth, just-picked look; avoid any mushy tips. Store in the refrigerator in a plastic bag for up to five days. Remove ends and strings just before cooking.

French Green Beans with Smoked Almonds
Olelo pa 'a Faith Ogawa, Dining by Faith

1   pound haricots verts (French green beans) or other green beans
¼   cup water
1-2 tablespoons butter
     Chopped smoked almonds
     Salt and pepper to taste

Trim stem end of beans and rinse. Place beans in a pot with the water and add a pinch or two of salt. Cover and cook for about three minutes over high heat. Cook to retain a slight crisp texture. Remove from heat and drain. Add butter and season to taste. Place the cooked beans on a platter and sprinkle with chopped smoked almonds.
     Serves 4.

Green Beans with Curry Seasoning
Fern Tomisato, Culinary Institute of the Pacific

1   pound green beans, cut 1½-inch length, stems removed
½   teaspoon ground cumin seeds
½   teaspoon ground coriander seeds
1   tablespoon curry powder
1½ teaspoons cooking oil
2   tablespoons minced round onions or shallots
3   tablespoons chopped mushrooms
1   teaspoon lemon juice
    Sliced almonds, optional
    Salt and pepper to taste

Steam green beans until crisp-tender and still bright green, about four minutes. Combine cumin, coriander and curry powder and toast in a dry skillet over medium heat until fragrance is released.

In a small skillet, heat oil over medium high heat. Add onions and mushrooms and cook until soft. Add lemon juice, green beans, and curry powder. Toss together and season with salt and pepper. Transfer to serving dish and garnish with almonds.

Serves 4.

GUAVA

Guavas have long been a fruit harvested in the wild – trees are pro-lific in forests and along roads everywhere in Hawai'i. On Kaua'i, guava has also been commercially planted, supplying processed fruit pulp and prepared foods to consumers.

The guava originated in tropical America and it has been in Hawai'i since the mid-1800s. It is a good source of vitamin C, especially in the rind. Guavas are most plentiful from June to October; fruit should be yellow in color and give to gentle pressure. If they are still green, store at room temperature until soft but refrigerate when ripe.

If you're lucky enough to obtain a batch of fresh guavas, here's how you can make your own guava puree concentrate for juice, pies, breads, sorbets and sauces.

Wash guavas and remove stem and bud ends. Cut each guava into four to six pieces. Measure guava chunks: for every four cups of guavas, add three-quarters to one cup of sugar. Toss together in a bowl, cover and refrigerate for four to six hours. Place guava and any liquid into a blender and puree until smooth. Pour into a strainer set over a bowl and press blended pulp through strainer with a spoon, leaving seeds behind. Discard seeds. Freeze the puree in one-cup portions.

Tropical Mimosa
Wendy Nakamura, Mariposa at Neiman Marcus

4   cups guava nectar
3   cups pineapple juice
¼   cup sugar
2   cups strong cool tea
1   bottle champagne

Combine all ingredients and chill thoroughly. Do not serve on ice.
Garnish with pineapple spears, lime slices and/or pineapple mint for a
delightful touch.
Serves 12.

Guava Yogurt Fruit Supreme
Kaua'i County Farm Bureau

¾   to 1 cup guava concentrate
1   package unflavored gelatin
2   tablespoons cold water
2   tablespoons hot water
1   pint plain or vanilla yogurt or 1 cup of each
2   cups fresh fruit such as papaya, orange, mango or other fruit in season,
    cut into bite-sized pieces

Soften gelatin in cold water. When it is soft, add hot water to dissolve
gelatin. Combine mixture with yogurt. Fold in guava concentrate.
Refrigerate until partially set. Fold in fruits and refrigerate until firm.
Serves 6.

HEARTS OF PALM

The edible heart of a peach palm is a mild-flavored, crisp morsel reminiscent of an artichoke heart. Cultivated along the Hāmākua Coast of the island of Hawai'i, the trees grow to six to eight feet in height before they are cut down by hand and stripped of their outer layers to reveal the heart at the core of the leaf cluster. The tree produces "keikis" which insure a harvestable stalk each year.

Hearts of palm can be simply sliced and dressed for a salad or sautéed in a little olive oil to top a salad or as a side dish. Use the thicker portion of the stalk for sautéing. Store hearts of palm in the refrigerator, wrapped in plastic, for up to a week.

Hearts of Palm, Avocado and Jicama Salad

Beverly Gannon, Hali'imaile General Store

Jicama (hih-kuh-muh) is also known as chop suey yam, Mexican potato or Mexican water chestnut. It's a tropical legume that produces a light brown, round taproot. The crispy white flesh is reminiscent of a water chestnut's and can be eaten raw or cooked. Choose roots whose skins are smooth, unblemished and thin. Store in a cool dry place; refrigerate after cutting, wrapping in plastic.

1   cup fresh hearts of palm, peeled, sliced into ¼-inch rounds
1   cup jicama, peeled and sliced thin
1   tablespoon extra-virgin olive oil
1   clove garlic, finely minced
1   cup mayonnaise
¼   cup ketchup
1   teaspoon sambal (chili sauce)
4   teaspoons sugar
2   tablespoons, plus 1 teaspoon lemon juice
2   tablespoons chopped cilantro
1   avocado, peeled and chopped
3   cups watercress, chopped
½   cup coarsely chopped toasted macadamia nuts
     Pinch of sea salt

Heat extra-virgin olive oil, in a small sauté pan over medium high heat. Add hearts of palm and sauté for one minute. Add garlic and 1 teaspoon lemon juice and sauté one more minute. Set aside to cool.

In a small bowl, whisk mayonnaise, ketchup, sambal, sugar and 2 tablespoons lemon juice. Add cilantro and mix.

In a bowl, place the hearts of palm, jicama and avocado. Toss mixture with just enough dressing to coat.

Place half a cup chopped watercress on six plates. Divide vegetable mixture evenly on top of watercress. Sprinkle macadamia nuts on top of salad. Serve with extra dressing on the side.

Serves 6.

HERBS

There's nothing that compares to fresh herbs, and you'll find a wide variety of them at farmers markets. Basil, thyme, marjoram, oregano, rosemary, dill, mint, cilantro, parsley, lemongrass, chervil –the list goes on. Buy them fresh, or better yet, get a potted plant and start your own herb garden!

When buying herbs, look for bright, fresh-looking leaves. Store them in their plastic packaging in the refrigerator until ready to use. Herbs should be used within a few days of purchase. Basil is especially fragile; try storing it with stems in a glass of water on your kitchen counter for up to two days. Herbs like thyme, marjoram, oregano and rosemary will dry well; allow to air dry for several days on your kitchen counter before placing in a storage container. Lemongrass can be chopped and frozen for storage.

BASIL shows up often in farmers markets, particularly sweet, or Italian basil and the darker and more anise-scented Thai basil. It's also very easy to propagate, so if you decide to grow your own, here are some tips for harvesting it. Pick it when you see the buds or the first open flower. This is when the herbs have the most oil. Pick the basil in midmorning when the leaves are dry—the herb is most fragrant then, and you'll avoid mold. Snip off whole branches to encourage new growth rather than picking leaves.

GINGER is one of Hawai'i's prized crops, grown mostly on the islands of Hawai'i and Kaua'i. The "root" used to add zest to Island dishes is actually a rhizome, a creeping horizontal stem that grows beneath the surface of the soil. Hawai'i-grown ginger has thin skin and less fiber than its mainland counterpart; look for firm, smooth skin with a light sheen. Be on the lookout for young ginger around August and September; it is ideal for pickling because it has less fiber and a milder flavor. Ginger is harvested annually—in Hawai'i, usually from December to February.

ROSEMARY is an herb that grows well in Hawaii, its needle like silver green leaves full of aroma and pine-like flavor. It's an herb that is native to the Mediterranean area and is frequently found in the kitchens of Italy and France. It's an herb that can be used in a variety of dishes but is especially well suited for lamb.

Use sprigs of rosemary like a brush to coat meats, fish and poultry with oil on the grill. Rosemary sprigs can also be placed on top of charcoal for flavor. To infuse the flavor of rosemary in cream sauces, simmer the leaves in milk or cream, then strain. Because of its strong flavor and resinous quality, it's a good idea to chop rosemary finely when applying it directly to foods. Use rosemary sparingly so as not to overwhelm.

Asian Green Sauce
Cheryl To, PacifiKool

This strong, fragrant sauce is great on grilled or sautéed chicken. It can also be used as a dip with chunks of bread, or heated in a pan and drizzled over cooked fish. The sauce will keep in the refrigerator for a week.

4   ounces fresh ginger, peeled and cut into ½-inch chunks
1   bunch cilantro, approximately 2 ounces, roots and stems removed
1   bunch green onions, approximately 2 ounces, roots removed
¼   cup peanut oil
2   teaspoons fresh lemon juice
2   tablespoons water
     Kosher salt to taste

Cut cilantro and green onions into one-inch lengths. Place them, with ginger, in a blender or food processor and process to a texture like pesto. Add peanut oil, lemon juice, and water. Mix, then add salt to taste.

Makes about 1 cup.

Linguine with Anchovies and Fresh Sweet Basil
Cheryl To, Owner PacifiKool

This is an easy, quick and simple dish. After you make it once, you won't have to use the recipe ever again. Have all your equipment and ingredients ready to go. This simple dish really shines when good-quality and very fresh ingredients are used.

1   pound of dry linguine (4 ounces per person)
½   cup good-quality olive oil
4-6 ounce jar of anchovies, packed in oil, roughly chopped
6-8 cloves of garlic, finely minced
12   medium-sized sweet basil leaves, cut into julienne
     Grated Parmesan
     Kosher salt

Have pasta bowls ready for serving. In a large pot of salted water, cook linguini. While pasta is cooking, heat olive oil in a large shallow pan. When the oil is hot, add garlic and cook, but don't let it brown. Quickly stir in anchovies and a little anchovy oil. Add a little kosher salt.

Drain pasta, reserving some pasta water. Toss pasta into the pan and add basil. Quickly incorporate all the ingredients, adding pasta water to moisten. Divide pasta among bowls. Garnish with a basil leaf and serve. Pass grated Parmesan and extra olive oil at the table.

Serves 4.

Butterflied Leg of Lamb

If you can find island grown lamb, by all means prepare it like this. Lamb is grown mostly on the island of Hawaii.

1   leg of lamb, bone removed and butterflied
6   cloves of garlic, coarsely chopped
2   tablespoons minced fresh rosemary
1   cup olive oil
1   tablespoon salt
     Juice of 2 lemons
     Freshly ground pepper

Combine marinade ingredients in a deep casserole or baking dish. Place lamb in marinade and turn several times to coat. Cover with plastic wrap and marinate for several hours in refrigerator or overnight.

Heat a grill to medium hot. Remove lamb from refrigerator 30 minutes before cooking. Cook lamb on grill for 30 to 45 minutes, depending on thickness, brushing with remaining marinade as it cooks. Test doneness with an instant read thermometer; at 140 to 145°F, lamb is medium done. Remove from grill and allow to rest for 10 to 15 minutes before slicing and serving.

LILIKOʻI

Lilikoʻi, the Hawaiian name given to the passion fruit, is one of the most popular locally grown fruits in Hawaiʻi. While you may not find it sold in the supermarket produce section, it is a common flavor of juice, jelly or syrup. It has a pleasant pucker-up tartness, and dressed with some sugar, its intense, almost citrus-like flavor is unsurpassed. It adds flair to glazes and sauces in both savory and sweet creations. Lilikoʻi chiffon pie is a quintessential favorite, and lilikoʻi curd is forever a winner.

In Hawaiʻi, passion fruit is grown on all islands. It grows easily from seed and harvests in winter. It is a good source of vitamin C. The fruit is a reddish purple or bright yellow and resembles a large egg. Inside, the yellow-orange flesh is soft, jelly-like and heavy with seeds. Ripen it at room temperature until the rind starts to soften and wrinkle. Store ripened fruit in the refrigerator or wrap it in plastic and freeze.

While passion fruit can be cut open and enjoyed as is, it is prized for its juice, which can be extracted by passing the pulp and seeds through a sieve or several layers of cheesecloth. Refrigerated, the juice will keep for about a week; frozen, up to six months. To sweeten it, use one part sugar to five parts juice by weight.

Passion Fruit Cheesecake with Macadamia Nut Crust
Elisabeth Iwata, Neiman Marcus

CRUST

1	cup all-purpose flour
½	cup unsalted butter, melted
½	teaspoon salt
3	tablespoons sugar
½	cup macadamia nuts, finely chopped and toasted

CHEESECAKE BATTER

2	pounds (four 8-ounce packages) cream cheese, at room temperature
2	pounds (32 ounces) mascarpone cheese*, at room temperature
2½	tablespoons cornstarch
2	cups sugar
½	cup passion fruit puree
5	eggs at room temperature
¾	cup whipping cream for garnish (optional)

For the crust, preheat oven to 350°F. Line the bottom of a 9-inch springform pan with foil.

Combine all crust ingredients in a small bowl and form dough—it will have a moist yet crumbly texture. Press dough into bottom of springform pan. Bake for 18 to 20 minutes until golden brown. Remove from oven and cool.

To make the batter: turn the oven down to 250° F. Soften the cream cheese using a mixer with a paddle attachment, mixing on lowest speed. Mix until smooth and creamy, scrape the bowl then add the mascarpone; mix until smooth and creamy. Keeping the mixer on low speed, add the cornstarch, sugar and passion fruit puree, one at a time; scrape the bowl well with each addition, preventing any lumps or unevenness from forming. Add the eggs one at a time, blending well after each addition; do not scrape the bowl or lumps will form. When the mixture is well blended, pour the batter into the springform pan, filling to a quarter of an inch below the rim.

Place pan in middle of oven. Place a pan of water on a rack below it. Bake for three hours. The cheesecake should be soft yet firm to the touch, and the sides should be pulling away from the pan. Remove from oven and cool for one hour. Chill for four hours or overnight before serving.

To serve, run a knife around the sides of the cake and gently detach the bottom of the pan. Garnish with whipped cream if desired and serve. The cheesecake will keep, wrapped and refrigerated for two to three days. Makes one 9-inch cake.

Mascarpone is an Italian sweet cheese, available in supermarkets and specialty food stores.

Passion Fruit Chiffon Pie

Joan Namkoong, Freelance Food Writer

⅔ cup passion fruit juice
1   envelope gelatin
¼   cup cold water
4   eggs, separated
1   cup sugar, divided
1   tablespoon lemon or orange zest (optional)
1   (9-inch) pie crust, baked
½   cup whipping cream

Soften gelatin in water. Set aside.

Beat egg yolks in top of double boiler until blended. Add half a cup of sugar and the juice; blend well and cook over simmering water until mixture is thick and coats the back of a spoon. Add gelatin and zest. Remove from heat and cool.

In a clean bowl, whip the egg whites with remaining sugar until stiff. Fold egg whites into passion fruit mixture and blend well. Fill pie shell, cover and refrigerate. When ready to serve, whip the cream until peaks form. Spread cream over the top and serve.

Serves 8.

Passion Fruit Curd
Elisabeth Iwata, Neiman Marcus

8   whole eggs
8   egg yolks
2   cups granulated sugar
1   cup passion fruit juice
½   pound unsalted butter, cut into 16 pieces
½   teaspoon lime zest

Using a whip, combine the eggs, yolks, sugar and juice in a large bowl. Set the bowl over a pot of simmering water and gradually reduce the mixture to a thick custard, stirring frequently. Blend in the chunks of butter, piece by piece. Strain the custard through a fine mesh sieve. Stir in the lime zest. Cover with plastic wrap to prevent a skin from forming and chill well.

Use the curd as a base for a meringue or cream pie, or as a condiment for scones.

Yields about one quart.

LOTUS ROOT

The lotus root, actually the underwater stem of a water lily, has been cultivated for over 3,000 years. It is a symbol of purity because its interior structure remains untainted even though it grows in muddy ponds. The interior tunnels of the sausage-like links form a unique, lace-like pattern not seen in any other vegetable.

Look for unblemished skins without soft or dark spots. Store in the refrigerator for up to two weeks. After cutting, lotus root needs to be put in water with a little lemon juice to keep it from turning brown.

Spicy Soy Lotus Roots
Olelo pa'a Faith Ogawa, Dining by Faith

1   pound peeled and cleaned fresh lotus roots, sliced to 1/8-inch thickness
2   tablespoons vegetable oil
1   Hawaiian chili pepper, minced, or ½ teaspoon garlic-chili sauce
1   teaspoon garlic, minced
1   teaspoon ginger, minced
2   tablespoons brown sugar
2   tablespoons soy sauce
2   tablespoons water
½   teaspoon shrimp dashi
    Salt to taste

Heat skillet and add the oil, then the chili pepper, garlic and ginger. Sauté at medium-high heat for about 20 seconds and then add the sugar, soy sauce, water and dashi; mix well. Add the lotus roots and stir. Cover for about two to three minutes and then uncover and stir; cook until liquid evaporates.

This dish can be served at room temperature or chilled. It is good as a pūpū or side dish.

Serves 6 to 8.

LYCHEE

Lychee and longan have long been backyard fruits in Hawai'i. But within the last decade these two luscious fruit, along with rambutan, have been commercially cultivated as well, on the Big Island and Kaua'i. Lychee, originally from Southeast Asia, peaks in the summer months, its clusters growing on tall stately trees. The brittle red shell of the oval fruit is peeled away to reveal a white translucent fruit with a sweet-tart grape-like flavor surrounding a single seed. Lychee should be stored in the refrigerator and can be frozen whole and unpeeled.

The longan is a smaller fruit, round in shape, with a yellow-brown exterior shell. The flesh surrounding the seed is sweet, less acidic than lychee, with a perfumy note; it resembles a peeled grape. Longan is often referred to as dragon's eye.

Rambutan is the hairy cousin of lychee and longan, larger in size with soft spines poking out of its bright yellow-red shell. Inside this oval fruit is a crisp, juicy fruit with pearly white flesh, falling somewhere between a lychee and a longan on the sweetness scale. To remove the thick outer shell of a rambutan, use a knife to cut around the middle and take off the top to reveal the fruit. Rambutan's red exterior turns black over time, but the fruit is still tasty inside. It stores well in the refrigerator.

Ginger-Stuffed Lychee
Kaua'i County Farm Bureau

2   dozen fresh lychee
1   (3-ounce) package cream cheese
1½   teaspoons lemon juice
½   teaspoon sugar
2   teaspoons crystallized ginger, minced

Peel lychee and remove seed. Combine remaining ingredients, blending well. Stuff lychee with mixture. Serve.
Makes 24.

Lychee Salsa
Olelo pa'a Faith Ogawa, Dining by Faith

This refreshing salsa is versatile and easy to prepare and can be made the night before. It is especially good with grilled shrimp, mahi mahi and ono. Add salad greens, and this dish turns into a nice attractive light salad.

¾   cup lychee with seed and skin removed, cut into small dice
⅓   cup orange, cut into small dice
⅓   cup ripe papaya, cut into small dice
1   tablespoon lemon juice
1   tablespoon mild honey
½   teaspoon to 1 teaspoon sambal sauce or chili garlic sauce
2   tablespoons red bell pepper, minced
1   teaspoon ginger, minced
2   pinches salt

Combine the all ingredients and marinate for at least one hour in the refrigerator. Garnish with fresh cilantro leaves and a lemon or lime slice.
Serves 4.

MACADAMIA NUTS

Macadamia nuts, or "mac nuts," make a great crunchy snack, a delicious ingredient for sweet and savory dishes and one of the healthiest cooking oils you can get. They can be added to soups, salads, sauces and stir-fries or used as a crunchy crust on your choice of meat, fish or chicken. But they really stand out when added to delicious desserts. The macadamia nut's unique buttery flavor is often the perfect complement to pies, cakes, cookies, breads and even ice creams.

Native to Australia, macadamia nut trees first arrived in Hawai'i in 1882. They were used primarily as ornamentals until the 1920s, when local farmers started harvesting the nuts for sale. Today, nearly all of Hawai'i's macadamia nuts come from about 700 farms on the Big Island.

The University of Hawai'i's John A. Burns School of Medicine published a study in 2000 about the benefits of macadamia nut products. A diet high in macadamia nuts (both oil and nuts) lowered participants' overall cholesterol levels and improved the body's ability to keep the "good" cholesterol and "bad" cholesterol in balance. Macadamia nuts are high in monounsaturated fats and low in saturated fats; they have no cholesterol and are high in omega-3 fatty acids and anti-oxidants. If you include mac nuts as part of a balanced diet and exercise regime, you could potentially reduce your chance of heart disease and high blood pressure. Nuts, yeah? Macadamia nuts are also pretty nutritious, containing protein, vitamin A, thiamine, riboflavin, niacin and iron.

For cooks, macadamia nut oil has some great benefits as well. It has a very long shelf life and a high smoke point (389° F). This, combined with its light flavor and clear appearance, makes macadamia nut oil great for sautéing, baking, roasting and salad dressings.

When buying macadamia nuts, look for a nice, creamy white color. If they are dark, it could mean they are over-roasted (and bitter) or rancid and spoiled. To keep them fresh, you should keep them in an airtight container in the refrigerator or the freezer. Properly stored, they can last up to a year.

Howard Yamasaki, Po'okela
Po'okela brand coffee and macadamia nuts, Honaunau, Hawai'i

Howard Yamasaki has an emphatic, one-word answer when he's asked what he likes about farming: "Independence." But the independence he and his wife, Chrystal, enjoy today as 26-year veterans of coffee and macadamia nut farming in Honaunau, South Kona, is hard won. He recalls having to work construction to make ends meet. During harvest season, he'd literally spend most of the night processing the coffee his hired hands had picked during the day. He still does that in season, but the rest of the time, he doesn't have to work quite that hard to farm his 12 acres.

Both Kona coffee and Hawai'i-grown macadamia nuts have an enviable reputation around the world, and Yamasaki notes that the volcanic soil, misty mornings and sunny afternoons in south Kona are tailor-made for the varieties that the University of Hawai'i helped develop. But both these crops face stiff competition from other growing areas that steeply undercut prices. Yamasaki says he learned long ago that the way to make it in coffee or macadamia nuts is to "integrate" – meaning the only person you sell to is the retail customer. No middlemen. Yamasaki grows, picks, processes, packages and markets almost everything he raises – online, at farmers markets and locally in Kona under the Po'okela brand. That way, he says, "I set the price."

Pineapple MacNut Bread
Abigail Langlas, Honolulu Coffee Company

8   ounces unsalted butter
2   cups granulated sugar
4   eggs
2   teaspoons vanilla
3   cups flour
2   teaspoons baking powder
1   teaspoons baking soda
1   teaspoons salt
½   cup buttermilk
2   cups crushed pineapple, drained
2   cups toasted macadamia nuts
    Zest of two oranges

In a mixing bowl, mix butter and sugar together until creamy. Add the eggs and vanilla and blend well.

Sift the dry ingredients together and add to butter/sugar mixture, alternating with buttermilk. Add pineapple and macadamia nuts. Divide mixture between two large greased loaf pans.

Bake for about an hour at 325° F in a convection oven, 350° F in a regular oven.

Makes two loaves.

MacNut Brittle

Abigail Langlas, Honolulu Coffee Company

4   cups macadamia nuts, toasted and still hot
2   pounds granulated sugar
½   cup water
½   cup corn syrup
½   cup unsalted butter
2   teaspoons vanilla
½   teaspoons salt
2   teaspoons baking soda, sifted

In a large, heavy saucepan, combine sugar, water, corn syrup and butter. Bring to a boil and continue to boil until mixture reaches a medium caramel color. Add vanilla, then salt and baking soda, then the hot nuts. Stir until the nuts are mixed in, but do not continue to stir after that, as it will deflate the brittle. Immediately pour mixture out onto a silicon baking mat or a greased cookie sheet. Pull apart as it cools.

Makes about four pounds.

Macadamia Chocolate Shortbread
Abigail Langlas, Honolulu Coffee Company

1½   cups roasted, chopped macadamia nuts
2¼   cups flour
⅜   teaspoon salt
1   cup plus 2 tablespoons unsalted butter
¾   cup granulated sugar
2¼   ounces milk
½   teaspoons almond extract
2   cups semi-sweet chocolate pieces

Preheat oven to 325° F. Grease a 9-inch x 13-inch baking pan and line with parchment or wax paper.

Sift flour and salt; set aside. Cream together butter and sugar. Add milk and almond extract and blend well. Add flour mixture and one cup of the macadamia nuts.

Spread dough onto baking pan and bake for 20-25 minutes. While still warm, spread chocolate pieces on top and return to oven. Heat for a minute or so until chocolate melts.

Spread chocolate evenly with spatula and sprinkle top with remaining nuts. Cut into squares.

Makes about 24 squares.

MANGO

There are countless varieties of mangoes grown in Hawai'i. The two major types found in stores are Haden (orange/red) and Pirie (yellow/green). You may also find Kietts, Tommy Atkins, and Kents. Use green Chinese and common mangoes for chutneys. Look for other varieties like white Pirie, Golden Glow, Wai'anae Beauty, and Mapulehu. All mangoes are rich in vitamin A and C. Mangoes are in season from April through September.

Look for firm fruit with a floral or fruity scent at the stem. Ripe mangoes vary in color from red and orange to yellow and green, depending on the type. Mangoes are harvested firm and ripen off the tree at room temperature. A ripe mango should be firm and will give slightly to pressure. Once ripe, it can be refrigerated for a few days.

How to cut a mango in neat cubes: Hold the fruit with its narrower profile facing you, stem end down. The pit runs the length of the fruit. Cut lengthwise along each side of the pit. You will have two large "cheek" pieces and the middle section with the pit. Slice the fruit off the pit. Then take one of the cheeks and make a crosshatch pattern through the fruit to the skin, but not through it. Then turn the cheek inside out and cut the cubes off the skin.

Or you can just peel and cut random pieces off the pit. Then stand over the sink eating the remaining flesh off the pit and let the juice stream down your face.

Mango Chutney
Kaua'i Farm Bureau

12   cups green mango slices
2   tablespoons rock salt
6   cups granulated sugar or 3 cups light brown sugar and 3 cups raw white sugar
3   cups vinegar
½   cup fresh ginger root, finely chopped
4   chili peppers, finely chopped and seeds removed
2   cloves garlic, finely chopped
3   cups raisins
1   cup sweet onion, sliced

Slice mangoes, sprinkle with salt and let stand overnight. Rinse and drain. Combine the sugar and vinegar in a large saucepan and bring to a boil. Add all the other ingredients and bring to a boil again. Then simmer for about one hour or until thickened. Pour into hot sterilized jars and seal immediately. Or cool, pour into clean containers, and refrigerate.

Makes about 3 quarts.

Mango Bread
Kaua'i Farm Bureau

1½ cups butter
2½ cups sugar
6   eggs
2   teaspoons vanilla extract
4   cups sifted all-purpose flour
1   teaspoon salt
4   teaspoons baking soda
3   teaspoons cinnamon
4   cups diced mango
1   cup chopped nuts (optional)

Preheat oven to 350° F.
Grease and flour five medium or four large loaf pans.
Cream butter, add sugar gradually and beat until fluffy. Add eggs one at a time and continue to beat. Add vanilla. Sift dry ingredients into egg mixture, alternating with the mango. Add nuts and blend well. Divide among pans; bake in medium pans 40-45 minutes, large pans one hour. Remove from the oven and cool.
Makes 4-5 loaves.

Mango Sweet Bread Pudding

Sandra Kunimoto, Director, Hawai'i State Department of Agriculture

1	cup fresh mango, cut into ½-inch dice
1½	pound loaf sweet bread, cut into 1-inch cubes
3	cups milk
½	cup butter, cut into 6-8 pieces
½	cup raw sugar
6	eggs, beaten
1	teaspoon vanilla
1	teaspoon cinnamon
½	cup pine nuts, toasted

Preheat oven to 350° F.

In a saucepan, over medium heat, warm milk. When milk is hot and bubbles begin to form around the edges, remove from heat. Add butter and sugar to the milk, stirring until butter is melted and sugar is dissolved. Cool.

Whisk eggs, vanilla and cinnamon into the egg mixture

Grease a 9-inch x 13-inch baking pan with butter. Place a third of the sweet bread in pan, top with half of the mango and nuts. Alternate layers, ending with bread on top. Pour milk/egg mixture evenly over bread; let stand a few minutes. Bake for 30 to 35 minutes. Remove from oven. Cool. Cut and serve.

Serves 12.

MELON

Melons have been grown for several millennia, dating back to the Egyptians. No doubt they enjoyed these sweet, juicy, perfumy fruits as much as we do today. Melons are really gourds, related to squash and pumpkin. In Hawaiʻi, cantaloupes (known in North America as muskmelons) and honeydews are grown mostly on the ʻEwa plain of Oʻahu where farmers are experimenting with different varieties. Watermelons – red, yellow and seedless varieties – are also grown in central Oʻahu and the North Shore, a refreshing and delightful treat in our tropical climate. Be sure to look for Thai watermelons, just five to seven pounds, small, crisp and sweet. The Yellow Doll is another must-try variety, fragrant and tasty but with a very short growing season. Low in calories and high in Vitamin A, C and potassium, any melon you pick is a "good one," nutritionally speaking.

Honeydews and cantaloupes should give to gentle pressure at the stem end; most of all, they should be fragrant. Melons should be heavy for their size. Allow them to ripen on your kitchen counter before refrigerating, especially honeydew.

Watermelons should be heavy for their size and sound hollow when thumped with your fingers. Whole melons will always have better flavor than cut ones.

Melon and Strawberries with Candied Mint Leaves
Sharon Kobayashi and Ruth Arakaki, Latitude 22

Asian cultures believe that melons cool the body's internal body temperature. They are 90 percent water, so it is easy to see why this could be true. When summer is at its hottest, the refreshing and clean flavors of this simple salad are an ideal addition to your table. Tart and fresh local strawberries complement the sweet juicy melon. The candied mint leaves sparkle like little jewels and add another cooling element to the fruit.

3   pounds cantaloupe, musk or honeydew melon, washed, peeled, seeded and cut into large dice

1   pint strawberries, washed and halved

12 to 15 candied mint leaves
(see Mint Syrup recipe from Great Lemonade recipe, page 58.)

In a large bowl, mix melon and strawberries. Top with mint leaves. Drizzle mint syrup to taste over fruit. Serve immediately.
Serves 6.

Cantaloupe and Bacon-Wrapped 'Ahi with Arugula
Sharon Kobayashi and Ruth Arakaki, Latitude 22

This entrée salad is perfect for a first course or summer lunch. 'Ahi is less expensive but leaner in the summer months, so bacon adds a welcome richness to the dish. The sweet musky cantaloupe balances the peppery arugula and salty bacon. If baby arugula is not available, substitute mixed greens or curly cress combined with baby spinach.

1½ pound cantaloupe (about ½ medium melon), peeled, seeded and sliced thin
8 slices bacon
1 pound 'ahi, blocked for sashimi (2 x 8-ounce blocks)
2 shallots, minced (about 4 tablespoons)
¾ cup balsamic vinegar
3 tablespoons soy sauce
1 sprig fresh rosemary (about 6-inch length)
2 tablespoons extra-virgin olive oil
6 ounces baby arugula (about 8 cups)

In a skillet, partially cook bacon, about five minutes. Reserve one tablespoon bacon drippings. Cool.

In the same pan, sauté shallots briefly, then add vinegar, soy sauce, and rosemary. Bring to a boil, then lower heat and simmer for three to five minutes to thicken slightly. Cool. Remove rosemary sprig from dressing and add olive oil and one tablespoon bacon drippings.

Lay four slices of bacon side by side on work surface. Place one sashimi block over bacon and wrap each piece of bacon around block. Secure bacon slices with toothpicks. Repeat with second block. Wrap blocks with plastic wrap and place in the freezer for 15-20 minutes.

In a heavy pan on medium heat, add 'ahi and brown on all sides until bacon is crisp. Remove from pan and drain on paper towels. Cut each block into four pieces (between bacon slices). Remove toothpicks.

In a bowl toss arugula with some of the dressing. Season with salt and pepper. Arrange cantaloupe slices on eight plates. Top with arugula and 'ahi. Serve with remaining dressing.

Serves 8 as a first course.

MOYA

The cherimoya, atemoya and soursop are usually all labeled "moya" for marketing convenience. All varieties have a thick, soft, inedible skin with shiny, watermelon-like seeds, and the sweet, creamy pulp combines the flavors of pineapple, papaya, passion fruit, banana, mango and lemon, all in one subtropical mouthful. The bumpy, scabby moya is among the earliest recorded New World fruits.

Moya turn a pale green or creamy yellow as they reach maturity. They should be picked when still firm and allowed to ripen at room temperature. A moya is ripe when it is soft to the touch and the stem end begins to split. Overripe fruit will begin to turn brown.

Store mature fruit above 55° F to prevent chilling injury to the skin and flesh. Ripe fruit will deteriorate quickly but can be stored at temperatures lower than 55° F for short periods. Ripe cherimoyas can be frozen and eaten like ice cream.

Cherimoyas are best served chilled, cut in half or quartered, and eaten with a spoon. The fruit can also be juiced and used to make delicious sorbets or purees. Chill and peel the fruit and remove all seeds.

All-Purpose Cherimoya Dessert Sauce

Barbara Holm, *Hawai'i Hospitality* Magazine

Ripe cherimoya flesh, seeds removed
Small chunks of banana
Canned, crushed pineapple, with juice
Cinnamon and nutmeg to taste

Blend all ingredients until nearly smooth, leaving a few chunks for texture. Best served immediately over ice cream or fruits.

Moya Sherbet

Barbara Holm, *Hawai'i Hospitality* Magazine

2   cups moya puree
1   (8-ounce) carton plain low-fat yogurt
¼   cup orange juice
2   tablespoons honey
1   teaspoon almond extract

Mix all ingredients to a creamy consistency. Pour into an 8-inch square pan and freeze until almost firm. Break mixture into large pieces and process in blender or food processor until fluffy but not thawed. Return mixture to pan or put into serving dishes and freeze until firm. Serves 4.

MUSHROOMS

Who would ever think we'd eat a fleshy fungus? That's what a mushroom is, and this earthy-flavored treat is simply delicious. Just about all the mushrooms we eat are cultivated rather than wild, and many exotic varieties are grown right here in Hawai'i.

At Hamakua Mushrooms on the Big Island, mushroom farming is state of the art in an environmentally controlled facility. Here, hon-shimeji, shiitake, gray cluster oyster, maitake, alii oyster (eryngii) and nameko mushrooms are grown, each with a distinctive flavor and texture that chefs and home cooks find intriguing. These mushrooms are best sautéed or grilled; but feel free to add them to soups, risottos and stir-fried dishes, too.

When buying mushrooms, freshness is critical. Look for firm, unblemished caps that are evenly colored. Avoid soft or damaged spots or dark bruises. Store mushrooms in the refrigerator but remove plastic wrapping if you're not going to use them right away. To best preseve their freshness, place mushrooms in a paper bag or on a paper towel-lined tray covered with a damp paper towel. Use mushrooms within a couple of days.

Mushrooms contain a lot of water, up to 90 percent. The longer you cook mushrooms, the more water they will lose, resulting in a chewier, denser texture and more intense flavor. To savor the mild nutty flavor of mushrooms, sauté them quickly over high heat and do not allow the moisture to be released.

Chinese Dressing with Hāmakua Mushrooms
Olelo pa'a Faith Ogawa, Dining by Faith

2   cups chicken thighs or breast; diced
1   pound ground pork
2   tablespoons vegetable oil
1   medium onion, diced
1   tablespoon ginger, minced
2   teaspoons garlic, minced
2   cups grey oyster mushrooms
2   cups alii mushrooms
8   pieces dried shitake mushrooms, soaked in water and diced
1   (8½-ounce) can bamboo shoots, diced
1   (5-ounce) can water chestnuts, sliced
1   (15½-ounce) can garbanzo beans, drained and rinsed
1   tablespoon cornstarch
3   tablespoons water
1   head mustard cabbage, blanched, cooled and sliced
    Salt to taste
    White pepper to taste
    Cilantro for garnish

SAUCE
¼   cup oyster sauce
½   cup liquid from soaking shiitake mushrooms
2   tablespoons sherry
1   tablespoon soy sauce
1   tablespoon raw sugar*
1   tablespoon red wine vinegar or light vinegar
1   teaspoon sesame oil

Heat a large sauté pan and add the oil and then the onions. Cook until onions are translucent and then add the ginger and garlic; stir well. Add the chicken and ground pork; cook for few minutes at a high temperature. Add the water chestnuts, bamboo shoots and beans and mix well.

In a small bowl mix the sauce ingredients, then add to the chicken mixture. Cook at medium temperature for five to seven minutes or until most of the liquid has evaporated. Add salt and pepper to taste.

Mix the cornstarch and water in a small bowl, then slowly add to the mixture and stir constantly until thickened slightly and the cornstarch is cooked. Remove from the heat and place on a platter. Garnish with mustard cabbage and cilantro leaves.

Serves 8-10.

White raw sugar is a natural sugar, less refined than granulated sugar and containing a little molasses. It is a Maui-grown and -processed product available at supermarkets throughout the state.

Mushroom Salad
Olelo pa'a Faith Ogawa, Dining by Faith

½   pound hon-shimeji mushrooms
4   cups water
¼   cup white wine vinegar
3   medium whole vine-ripened tomatoes cut into ½-inch cubes
6-8 fresh basil leaves cut into thin julienne slices
¼   cup olive oil
1   teaspoon minced garlic
1   teaspoon grated lemon rind
2   tablespoons lemon juice
1   teaspoon fish sauce
    Salt and pepper to taste

In a medium pot, bring water to a boil. Add salt to taste and vinegar. Add mushrooms and simmer for five minutes. Drain, rinse and cool.

In a bowl combine tomatoes, basil and mushrooms. Add remaining ingredients and toss. Garnish with fresh basil leaves. Refrigerate before serving.

Serves 4.

Chicken Fettuccine and Shiitake Mushroom Casserole
Rebecca Schillaci, Hali'imaile General Store

¼   cup butter
¼   cup flour
1   cup milk
1   cup chicken broth
¼   cup sherry
2   cups sour cream
8   ounces egg fettuccine, cooked and drained
1   large chicken, cooked and boned
½   cup chopped onion, sautéed in 1 teaspoon butter
1   cup sliced shiitake mushrooms, sautéed in 1 tablespoon butter
½   cup sliced black olives
¼   cup sliced water chestnuts
1   cup fresh spinach leaves, cooked and squeezed dry
1   tablespoon dried tarragon leaves
1   cup grated Monterey Jack cheese
½   cup grated Parmesan cheese
    Salt and pepper to taste

Preheat oven to 300° F.

For the sauce, melt butter and flour together in a saucepan, stirring constantly. Add milk and chicken broth and continue to cook and stir until thickened. Add the sherry and sour cream and blend well. In a large bowl toss together pasta and one cup of sauce.

Add chicken, onion, mushrooms, olives, water chestnuts, spinach and tarragon. Toss together and add remaining sauce. Season with salt and pepper. Transfer to a baking dish or casserole; top with cheeses and bake 30-40 minutes.

Serves 6.

ONIONS

Sweet onions grown on Maui and O'ahu are available through most of the year. Nothing quite compares to the delicious, spicy crunch of raw, sweet onions or the savory aroma and flavor when onions are cooked.

When you buy onions, the best value is found in an onion heavy for its size with dry, papery skin and no graying, soft spots, strong odors, or moistness.

Store onions in a dark, dry, well-ventilated space for up to five weeks. Tightly wrap cut onions, refrigerate and use within four days. Toss sprouting onions. Chop onions in advance and store in the freezer. Prevent tearing by freezing for 20 minutes before chopping or wear goggles.

The curative powers of onions are amazing. They are a good source of vitamin B and vitamin C and trace minerals, and are low in sodium. Numerous studies show onions can help maintain good health.

Sweet Onion Tartlets
Carol Nardello, Sub Zero/Wolf

2 large sweet onions, thinly sliced
2 packages frozen mini filo cups
1 tablespoon butter
1 tablespoon olive oil
1 bay leaf
1 tablespoon fresh thyme
½ pound Swiss cheese, shredded
   Salt and pepper

Preheat oven to 375° F.

Arrange filo cups in a single layer on sheet pan. In a skillet, melt butter with oil over medium heat. Add onions and bay leaf. Season with thyme, salt and pepper. Cook onions until caramel colored, about 20 minutes.

Place a scant spoonful of onions into tart shells. Top onions with cheese and bake for 10 minutes. Serve hot.

PAPAYA

P apaya is one of Hawai'i's premier fruits, one that's good for you and an excellent source of vitamins C and A. Along with just 80 calories, you get nearly twice the amount of vitamin C an adult needs each day and three-fourths of the vitamin A requirement in half a papaya. As the fruit ripens, the vitamin C content increases, so it's best to eat fruit that is fully ripe.

Buy fruit according to its color. As a papaya turns yellow from the bloom end toward the stem end, ripeness increases. Most varieties are ready to eat when they are half yellow. Buy fruit at varying stages of ripeness so they will be ready to eat throughout the coming week. Ripen at room temperature and refrigerate when the desired color is achieved.

Papayas are best eaten on their own with a squeeze of fresh lemon or lime. To use the seeds of the papaya, prepare the following dressing:

Papaya Seed Dressing
College of Tropical Agriculture and Human Resources
University of Hawai'i at Mānoa, Cooperative Extension Service

1½   tablespoons fresh papaya seeds
1   cup salad oil
⅓   cup tarragon vinegar
1   tablespoon fresh lime juice
2   tablespoons sugar
½   teaspoon salt
½   teaspoon dry mustard
2   teaspoons minced onion

Place all ingredients except papaya seeds in a blender, cover and blend at high speed for two minutes. Add papaya seeds and blend until mixture is thick and the papaya seeds look like ground pepper. Transfer to a container and chill.

Makes one and a half cups.

Papaya Salsa

Sandra Kunimoto, Director, Hawai'i State Department of Agriculture

This fresh papaya salsa is delicious with tortilla chips or as an accompaniment to char-broiled steak or chicken.

1   large papaya, seeds removed, peeled and cut into 1/3-inch cubes
½   medium sweet onion, cut into ¼-inch dice
2   large Anaheim chilis,* roasted, peeled and cut into ¼-inch pieces
1   tablespoon balsamic vinegar
¼   teaspoon red chili flakes
   Salt to taste

In a bowl, toss together all ingredients. Adjust seasonings, adding more chili pepper flakes if desired. Refrigerate until ready to serve. Makes about 2 cups.

*You can also use canned Anaheim/green chilis.

Melvin Matsuda, Matsuda-Fukuyama Farm
(Kahuku Brand Haleiwa), Kahuku, Oʻahu

Ask Melvin Matsuda the hardest part about being a farmer, and he pauses for a while. Then he smiles and says, "The hardest part? That's a tough question. Every day there's something different, and there are so many aspects to the work – and so many people, from my wife to my daughter, my business partner and our employees who cover the areas." In essence, what Matsuda is trying to say is he finds his work challenging and enjoyable.

Born into a farming family in Kahuku, Matsuda was working with his dad while he was still in high school. "I took a couple years off," he says, "but this is what I wanted to do."

With his partner, Clyde Fukuyama, Matsuda concentrates on running their two properties in Kahuku and Haleʻiwa. "Our principle crops are papaya, apple bananas and mangoes, and we also grow long eggplant and taro leaves at the Kahuku farm," he explains.

Long-time farm enthusiasts are aware that the biggest problem facing North Shore farmers has always been theft – and Matsuda Fukuyama Farms is no stranger to the audacity of local burglars. "It's kind of the cost of doing business here," says Matsuda, with some resignation. "I don't think the problem is ever going to go away; we just do what we can to cope with it."

But for this dedicated family farmer, who takes pride in the fact that his wife and 27-year-old daughter, Kylie, are as passionate about the business as he is, not theft, nor wind, nor rain, can keep him from doing what he loves. "You know," he says, with a smile, "it's a lot of fun working on a farm."

PERSIMMON

The cool slopes of Haleakalā on Maui and Kamuela on the Big Island are ideal growing areas for a prized fruit that originated in China, the persimmon. The bright orange, tomato-shaped spheres are a delightful addition to our fruit selections during the last few months of each year. While mainland imports are plentiful, Island-grown persimmons have lots of sweetness.

Hachiya, maru and fuyu varieties are grown in Hawai'i. Hachiya is more heart shaped and must be eaten when soft. Maru persimmons are more yellow in color and often have brown spots, indicating high sugar content. This crunchy variety must be cured with a blast of cold to remove the astringency in the skin. Fuyu is another crunchy variety, well liked for its sweetness.

Eat persimmons out of hand or slice them up into a salad. Wrap a slice of persimmon with a slice of prosciutto. Soups, puddings and desserts can include this delightful fruit. Also look for dried persimmons, which help to extend the all-too short season.

Persimmon Salsa

Jackie Hashimoto, Hashimoto Farm, Kula, Maui

3   fuyu or maru persimmon, peeled and diced
1   cup fresh pineapple, diced
¼   cup chopped sweet onion
2   tablespoons chopped mint
     Salt to taste

Combine ingredients in a bowl. Refrigerate until ready to serve.
Makes about 3 cups.

Persimmon Bread

Jackie Hashimoto, Hashimoto Farm, Kula, Maui

2   cups persimmon, peeled and diced
2   cups flour
2   teaspoons baking soda
1   tablespoon ground cinnamon
½   teaspoon kosher salt
1½   cups raw white sugar
3   eggs, beaten
¾   cup vegetable oil
1   teaspoon vanilla
¾   cup diced macadamia nuts

Preheat oven to 350°F. Prepare two 8-inch x 4-inch loaf pans.
In a bowl, combine flour, baking soda, cinnamon and salt.
In a large mixing bowl, whisk together sugar, eggs, oil and vanilla. Add persimmon and gently mix together. Add dry ingredients and blend well. Mix in nuts. Pour into prepared pans and bake for about 45 minutes.
Makes 2 loaves.

Persimmon Sour Cream Coffee Cake

Jackie Hashimoto, Hashimoto Farm, Kula, Maui

1 cup persimmon pulp	STREUSEL TOPPING
⅓ cup brown sugar	½ cup flour
2 cups plus 1 tablespoon flour	½ cup sugar
2 teaspoons baking powder	½ teaspoon cinnamon
½ teaspoon baking soda	¼ cup butter
½ teaspoon salt	
½ cup butter at room temperature	
1 cup sugar	
1 teaspoon vanilla	
2 eggs	
1 cup sour cream	

Preheat oven to 350°F. Grease and flour a 9-inch by 3-inch spring-form pan; set aside.

Combine persimmon, brown sugar and one tablespoon flour; set aside.

In a medium bowl, stir together flour, baking powder, baking soda and salt. In a large bowl, cream the butter and sugar. Beat in vanilla. Add eggs, one at a time, beating well after each addition. Add flour mixture and sour cream, alternating, beating until combined after each addition.

For topping, combine flour, sugar, and cinnamon in a bowl. Cut in butter until mixture resembles coarse crumbs. Set aside.

Spread half the batter into prepared pan, building a one-inch rim of batter around edges of pan. Spoon persimmon mixture into center of pan. Spoon remaining batter in small mounds, covering the persimmon mixture and spreading to the edges. Sprinkle streusel over batter. Bake for one hour or until toothpick inserted in cake near center comes out clean. Filling will sink a little as coffee cake bakes. Remove from oven and cool in pan on a wire rack for 10 minutes. Loosen and remove sides of spring-form pan. Cool completely on wire rack.

Serves 12.

PINEAPPLE

The pineapple is a symbol of Hawai'i, a fruit that was brought to the Islands on Spanish sailing ships and has been grown here since the mid-1800s. But it wasn't until the twentieth century that pineapple became Hawai'i's second-largest crop, next to sugar, when Dole and Del Monte offered canned pineapple to the world.

Pineapple is a fruit that must be picked ripe, making it difficult to transport over long distances. That's why the canned pineapple industry took off in the Islands, before the days of air transportation. Today the remaining pineapple plantations in Hawai'i produce fruit to be eaten fresh, both here and on the West Coast.

Choose pineapples that are large and heavy for their size. There should be a sweet pineappley aroma and dark green fresh leaves; good color indicates sweetness. The Cayenne variety was long the staple of pineapple growers but today the sweet, less acidic Gold varieties are more available in the market. Watch for white Sugarloaf pineapples from Kaua'i and the Hawaiian Gold variety from the Big Island, both sweet with a robust flavor.

If you buy a pineapple at room temperature, keep it that way until you're ready to eat it. If you buy a chilled pineapple, keep it chilled. Temperature changes can cause dark spots to develop. Once cut, pineapple should be eaten within three to four days.

Pineapple Ginger Chicken Stir Fry
Maui Pineapple Company

2 cups fresh pineapple chunks
2 teaspoons peanut oil
1½ pounds boneless, skinless chicken breasts, cubed
1 tablespoon molasses
2 tablespoons fresh lime juice
¼ teaspoon red pepper flakes
8 green onions, cut into 2-inch pieces
¼ cup minced crystallized ginger

In a large skillet or wok, heat the oil over high heat. Add chicken and sauté until firm and well browned, about six minutes. Remove chicken and set aside.

Add pineapple and molasses to the pan and stir-fry until the pineapple is brown and tender. Stir in the lime juice, red pepper flakes, green onions and chicken.

Cook for another five minutes or until chicken is fully cooked and green onions are bright green. Add ginger and toss. Serve at once over rice.

Serves 4.

Pineapple Chutney
Kaua'i County Farm Bureau

4   cups chopped fresh pineapple
1   (15-ounce) package golden raisins
1½   cups vinegar
1½   cups brown sugar
1   tablespoon salt
2   tablespoons minced ginger
2   tablespoons minced garlic
1   medium round onion, chopped (optional)
2-3 Hawaiian chili peppers, seeded and minced
1   cup chopped macadamia nuts (optional)

In a large saucepan, combine all ingredients except the nuts. Bring to a boil, lower the heat and simmer until pineapple is tender, about 30 minutes or more.

Continue to cook until chutney thickens to desired consistency. Add nuts, if desired. Remove from heat and fill clean jars. Cool, cover and refrigerate.

Makes 6 cups.

Grilled Pineapple and Citrus Fruit

Barbara Holm, *Hawai'i Hospitality* Magazine

Serve with a scoop of ice cream or sorbet or as a grilled dessert.

1 pineapple, skin removed, cut into wedges and core removed
1 cantaloupe, seeds removed, peeled and cut into wedges
1 honeydew melon, seeds removed, peeled and cut into wedges
2 limes, cut in half
1 orange, cut in half
2 sprigs mint

Preheat a grill to medium. Place all fruit on grill, cut side down. Turn the pineapple and melon wedges once to grill both sides. Grill a few minutes until the fruits are lightly browned and the natural sugars are caramelized.

Remove fruit from the grill. Squeeze grilled limes and oranges over pineapple and melon. Garnish with fresh mint sprigs and serve.

Serves 8.

PORK

F eral pigs roam all of the Hawaiian islands, and it's a common sight to see intrepid hunters and their dogs heading out to bag one of these large, fierce creatures. But if you're hesitant about the possibility of getting gored and don't have any friends to keep you supplied, don't worry. You can still enjoy Island-fresh pork, courtesy of the several farms that raise pigs on Kaua'i. Pork's natural sweetness marries especially well with Island fruits.

Roasted Pork Tenderloin with Sweet Onion Marmalade
Carol Nardello, Sub Zero/Wolf

2 (1-pound) pork tenderloins
2 tablespoons olive oil
   Salt and freshly ground pepper

ONION MARMALADE
1 pound sweet onions, sliced
2 tablespoons olive oil
3 cloves garlic, minced
2 tablespoons balsamic vinegar
¼ cup brown sugar
2 tablespoons tomato paste
½ teaspoon ground ginger
⅛ teaspoon ground cloves
⅛ teaspoon ground nutmeg

Preheat oven to 350° F.

Heat oil in large ovenproof skillet over medium heat. Season pork generously with salt and pepper. Add pork to skillet and brown on all sides; about eight minutes total. Transfer skillet to oven. Roast pork until thermometer inserted into center registers 150°F, about 15 minutes. Remove pork from oven; let rest 10 minutes. Slice pork half an inch thick. Serve with onion marmalade.

To make the marmalade: In a sauté pan over medium-high heat, heat olive oil. Sauté onions and garlic about 10 minutes or until they just begin to turn brown. Add vinegar and sugar and cook five minutes, stirring often. Stir in tomato paste and spices and cook for a few minutes to blend flavors. Serve warm.

To improve flavor, prepare marmalade a day or two in advance. Cover and refrigerate. Re-warm before serving.

Sserves 4-6.

Ushi Kaneshiro, M&H Kaneshiro Farms
Ōma'o, Kaua'i

Ushi Kaneshiro came to Hawai'i from Okinawa in 1909 to work on a sugar plantation on O'ahu. Six years later he relocated to Koloa Plantation on Kaua'i. Looking for a way to support his family of eight sons, Kaneshiro started a pig farm. Today a 13-acre site in Ōma'o accommodates 1,500 hogs, and the fourth generation is now in place to carry on the farming tradition.

Pig farming is not without its challenges, as health and environmental rules and regulations have become more stringent in recent years. But on the good side, the Kaneshiros maintain a healthy herd that is disease free and good for breeding. Their delicious pork is available at hotels, restaurants and supermarkets – and no doubt on Kaua'i's finest lū'au tables.

RADISH

The lowly – but extremely healthful – radish is the root of a plant related closely to mustard, another surprisingly nutritious plant. It's generally used as a garnish or salad ingredient because of its mild to peppery flavor and clear, bright coloration.

Look for radishes that are firm, unblemished and bright in color. The most important indicator to look for is a fresh top, as a wilted top is the first sign of an aging radish.

Radishes are best stored in a plastic bag with holes in the bag. Wipe with a damp paper towel prior to storing. Ideal temperature is 50° F; however, you can keep them in your refrigerator for up to a week

To clean, scrub the radishes under cold running water. Cut off tops. Soak radishes in ice water for an hour or two for extra crispness.

A number of different radishes are available. Daikon is a radish that looks a lot like a cross between a white carrot and a turnip. Radish sprouts are a great addition to salads and sandwiches. Radishes can also add zip to vegetable juices.

Yucatecan Radish Salsa

Nancy Thomas, Chambers and Chambers

This radish salsa is the Yucatecan version of the classic Mexican tomato salsa and is bursting with flavor and texture. Serve it as a dip with tortillas chips or as the perfect complement to fajitas or grilled meats.

3 medium Roma tomatoes, diced
8 radishes, diced
2 tablespoons red onion, minced
1 avocado, peeled and diced
3-4 sprigs cilantro, chopped
1 teaspoon salt
½ teaspoon pepper
1 habañero* chili, minced
   Juice of 2 limes

Mix all ingredients except chili together. Add chili gradually, to taste. The spice will intensify slightly as salsa sits and flavors meld, so take that into account. Salsa can be stored in an airtight container in refrigerator for 7 to 10 days. When making it in advance, add avocado shortly before you plan to serve to avoid discoloration.

Makes about 3 cups.

*Habañeros grown in Hawai'i are the most potent of the chilies. Wear gloves when chopping them and be careful not to touch your eyes, face or lips. Habañero chilies range greatly in heat level and can go up to fiery, so add the chili gradually, about an eighth at a time, tasting for preferred level of spiciness.

SALAD GREENS

Unlimited choices of salad greens abound: buttery, spicy, curly, multi-colored. Once you have selected your leafy salad components, the next step is to wash them properly. A major priority in this procedure is to avoid bruising the leaves. Achieve this by soaking the leaves in cold water rather than rinsing under running tap water.

After soaking, gently swish the leaves to remove the grit and dirt. Lift them out gently and drain to dry. Heartier leaves can be put into a salad spinner to remove the water; tender, more delicate leaves need to rest on towels and be patted dry. Discard imperfect leaves. Try to wash the greens right before using, but if you must store cleaned leaves, wrap them in paper towels and place them in plastic bags. Remove as much air as possible from the bags, seal tightly and refrigerate until ready to use.

Preparing the perfect salad involves balancing shapes, colors, textures and flavors of greens. Additions of other vegetables, protein, grains, and garnishes enhance the presentation and taste.

Nutritionists consider dark greens like romaine, mustard greens, curly endive, red oak leaf lettuce, and other dark greens super foods. Darker leaves have seven times the cancer-fighting carotenoids of iceberg lettuce. More than half of those carotenoids are lutein and zeaxanthin, which protect your eyes against macular degeneration. Two cups of mixed greens counts as one or more daily servings of greens.

Tips for Dressing a Salad

- For mellow greens with a mild flavor, like Boston, Bib, red and green leaf, red oak, lolla rossa and iceberg, use a simple dressing like red wine vinaigrette.
- For spicy greens like arugula, watercress, mizuna and baby mustard, use a bolder dressing, perhaps one with mustard, balsamic vinegar and shallots.
- For bitter greens such as escarole, chicory, Belgian endive, radicchio, frisee and dandelion greens, use a creamy, robust vinaigrette.

ARUGULA is plentiful in the farmers markets, and salad lovers count themselves fortunate. This fabulous green adds a unique blast of flavors: bitter, sharp and peppery, coupled with a crisp texture. The intensity of the flavor changes with the growing conditions and maturity of the plant. Use the young, paler leaves in salads and the mature, darker, full-flavored leaves for cooking (which tames the bitterness considerably) to bring depth and character to pastas and sautés.

While the flavor is bold, the leaves are delicate and should be handled gently to avoid bruising during washing. Soaking and changing the water several times while swishing the leaves removes the sandy grit and debris. Dry carefully on towels or in a salad spinner.

Geoff Haines, Waipoli Hydroponic Greens
Kula, Maui

Geoff Haines wants to perpetuate agriculture on Maui, and as a partner in Waipoli Hydroponic Greens, he's doing just that.

Since 1997, Haines and his partner Paul Singleton have been providing the state with a variety of hydroponically grown greens – butter, baby romaine, green and red oak leaf lettuces, bok choi and watercress. Their delicate product is found in many supermarkets and restaurants on Maui and O'ahu.

Waipoli Hydroponic Greens has three acres with 88,000 plants growing year-round. Consistency and quality of product are foremost among the farmers concerns, while conserving land and water resources is equally important in their operations.

It's not easy being a lettuce farmer (or any farmer, for that matter). For Haines the challenge is dealing with a very tight market window for a highly perishable product. Thrice-weekly harvests, about 4,500 pounds a week, must be sold within a few days. But Haines is a true farmer at heart, and the enjoyment of working outdoors while earning a living is worth all the hassles.

Arugula Salad with Fresh Figs, Prosciutto and Parmigiano
Carol Nardello, Sub Zero/Wolf

½   pound arugula
2   tablespoons fig balsamic vinegar
½   teaspoon Dijon mustard
6   tablespoons extra-virgin olive oil
6   ounces prosciutto, sliced
6   firm-ripe green or purple figs, quartered
4   ounces Parmigiano-Reggiano, shaved
    Salt and fresh ground pepper

To make the dressing, in a small bowl, whisk together vinegar, mustard, salt, and pepper to taste. In a slow stream, whisk in oil until it emulsifies.

Discard stems from arugula and place leaves in a bowl. Roll up prosciutto slices and roughly chop. In a skillet with a little olive oil, sauté prosciutto until light brown and crisp. Dress arugula with half of the vinaigrette and mound on six plates. Arrange figs and crispy prosciutto on top and garnish with Parmigiano-Reggiano shavings. Pass remaining vinaigrette.

Serves 4.

Arugula Salad with Grilled Italian Sausage and Potatoes
Carol Nardello, Sub Zero/Wolf

3   cups arugula
1   pound hot sausage such as Portuguese, Andouille or Italian
1   pound small boiling potatoes, cut into ¼-inch slices
1   medium red onion, cut into ½-inch slices
½   cup roasted red peppers, cut in ¼-inch strips
6   tablespoons extra-virgin olive oil
2   tablespoons red wine vinegar
    Salt and pepper

Preheat grill.

Toss potatoes, onion and red pepper with two tablespoons olive oil, salt and pepper. Put oiled vegetables and sausages onto hot grill and cook through, turning occasionally, about 10 minutes. Remove from grill and place in a large bowl. Add arugula and toss together with remaining olive oil and vinegar. Season with salt and pepper and serve.

Serves 6.

Kurt and Pam Hirabara, Hirabara Farm
Waimea, Hawai'i

A special three-acre parcel in the Pu'ukapu district of Waimea on the Big Island produces more than dozen varieties of baby lettuces that are used in some of Hawai'i's award-winning restaurants and hotel dining rooms. This success is really quite amazing, considering the fact that farmers Kurt and Pam Hirabara admit they thought they were doing something wrong when they tasted their first test crops of lettuces. The problem? They had flavor. "We pulled the crops out and threw them away. We thought lettuce was supposed to be mild and watery."

The Hirabaras are first-generation farmers who have been at it for more than a dozen years. In addition to baby lettuces and succulent baby romaine, they also grow a number of specialty crops, like baby fennel, artichokes, celeriac and fingerling potatoes. For them, the best part about being a farmer is that "we are producing food, and the better job we do, the better the food is."

Dean Okimoto, Nalo Farms
Waimanalo, O'ahu

Just as there are celebrity chefs in America, Dean Okimoto is the "celebrity farmer" of Hawai'i. As the chief farmer and businessman behind Nalo Farms, Inc., Okimoto services over 120 restaurants on O'ahu, Kaua'i and Maui with his proprietary mix of premium lettuces known as "Nalo Greens," grown on his three-acre farm in Waimanalo on O'ahu.

Okimoto has been supplying his premium salad mix for just over a decade. Restaurateur and celebrity chef Roy Yamaguchi was his first customer, as well as the man who helped Okimoto expand his business. Once Okimoto could supply a quality product on a consistent basis, many others were clamoring to buy his assortment of fresh herbs and salad greens.

Prior to his success as a supplier to restaurants, Okimoto struggled on the family farm started by his father in the 1950s. Okimoto, born and raised in Hawai'i and a graduate of 'Iolani School in Hawai'i and the University of Redlands in California, returned to the family farm in 1983 after several years in the business arena in Honolulu. Hydroponic lettuces and herbs sustained the farm for about six years, but it was his connection with Yamaguchi that solidified his business as a farmer.

Okimoto started a second company, Local Island Fresh Edibles, Inc., that provides a marketing and distribution service for other farmers and their products. Premium tomatoes, eggplant, corn, romaine lettuce and other items are among the fresh products delivered to restaurants via this company.

In addition to running his business, Okimoto has engaged farmers on other islands and taught them to grow the Nalo Greens salad mix. Okimoto also serves as president of the Hawai'i Farm Bureau Federation.

Butter Lettuce Salad
Celia Haines, Maui County Farm Bureau

1   head butter lettuce, rinsed and chilled
2   large Hawaiian oranges
1   medium sweet onion, thinly sliced in rings and separated
1   cup pitted ripe olives

DRESSING
½   cup vegetable oil
¼   cup white wine vinegar
2   tablespoons sugar
1   teaspoon Dijon-style mustard
½   teaspoon paprika
½   teaspoon salt

Peel oranges and slice into thin rounds. Combine with onion in a shallow glass bowl. Whisk together dressing ingredients, blending well. Pour dressing over oranges and onions. Cover and chill for several hours.

When ready to serve, tear lettuce into bite-size pieces. Lift oranges and onions from dressing and add to lettuce. Add olives and toss well. Drizzle with a little more dressing, if desired. Serve immediately.

Serves 4.

SOY BEANS

Fresh Hawai'i-grown soybeans have great flavor, texture and color. Look for firm green pods with no discoloration. Soybeans should be kept refrigerated until used, and they will usually keep for two to three days. They need no ripening, as they must always be boiled before being consumed. To prepare soybeans, boil or steam in the pod for 15 minutes or until tender. Cooked soybeans will likewise keep in the refrigerator for two to three days, or you can freeze them in or out of the pod for later use.

A half-cup serving of cooked soybeans contains 127 calories, 5.8 grams of fat, 3.8 grams of fiber, 11 grams of protein and 10 grams of carbohydrates – a hefty serving of nutrients in a small package.

Minty Soy Bean Salad
Lori Wong, Culinary Consultant

3   pounds soybeans, cooked and shelled
3   green onion stalks, washed and finely chopped
1   bunch mint, cut into a chiffonade
1   (16-ounce) can water chestnuts, sliced

DRESSING
¼   cup mayonnaise
1   teaspoon salt
¼   cup sour cream
1   teaspoon white pepper

Place soybeans, green onions, mint and water chestnuts in a bowl. Whisk mayonnaise, sour cream, salt and pepper. Combine with other ingredients. Chill for one hour before serving.
Serves 8.

Soybean "Hummus"
Joan Namkoong, Free Lance Food Writer

The beautiful green color of soybeans is especially appetizing in this simple and delicious mixture, which can be served with crackers or raw vegetables.

1   pound fresh soybeans, cooked and shelled
1   clove garlic
⅓   cup extra-virgin olive oil
     Juice of 1 lemon or lime
     Salt to taste

Puree soybeans, lemon juice and garlic in food processor, adding olive oil. Add salt to taste and blend, adding more olive oil for a thinner consistency, if desired. Serve with crackers or raw vegetables.
Makes about 1 cup.

SPINACH

Dark, leafy spinach grows well in cool climates in Hawai'i. Depending on the variety, spinach leaves can be flat or curly; flat-leaf and baby spinach are best used for salads, while the more fibrous curly varieties work better steamed or sautéed.

Spinach leaves should be vibrant green in color and crisp. Avoid spinach with wilted or yellowing leaves, a slimy feel or a musty odor. An unpleasant mineral or metallic taste, which becomes more pronounced with cooking, is an indication of deterioration and lack of freshness. The size of the leaf is not an indication of tenderness; large leaves can be just as succulent and tender as smaller ones.

Spinach is best stored loosely wrapped in a plastic bag for three to five days. To retain the vegetable's phytochemicals and vitamins, the ideal storage temperature is 39° F. After five days there is significant loss of nutrients.

Spinach is grown in sandy soil. To remove the sand and grit, thoroughly rinse the leaves in several changes of cold water. The best method is to fill a large bowl with cold water, swish the spinach around and let the sediment sink to the bottom. Repeat till the bottom of the bowl is free of dirt and grit. For salads, the stringy stems can be removed by gently pulling the stem away from the leaf.

Drop a handful of raw spinach into omelets, ramen, or even canned soups. Chop and lightly sauté several cups of spinach to add to meatloaf or hamburger patties, or use as a pizza topping.

Spinach is exceptionally rich in carotenoids, including beta-carotene and lutein, and also contains quercetin, a phytochemical with antioxidant properties. The antioxidant carotenoids are much easier for your body to absorb in cooked versus raw spinach. Spinach is rich in vitamins and minerals, particularly folate (folic acid), vitamin K, magnesium, and manganese; it also contains more protein than most vegetables. Spinach has 40 calories per 1½-cup serving.

Cold Udon Salad with Spinach and Mushrooms
Melanie Kosaka, First Daughter Mediaworks

11	ounces spinach
8	ounces dry udon noodles
8	ounces fresh shiitake mushrooms, sliced
8	ounces fresh oyster mushrooms, sliced
2	tablespoons olive oil
1	tablespoon fresh lemon juice
1	cup grated daikon
6	shiso leaves, chopped
	Red pickled ginger
	Nori strips, extra fine
	Salt and pepper to taste

DRESSING

¼	cup mirin
1	tablespoon sugar
1	cup dashi-no-mono*
⅓	cup soy sauce
2½	tablespoons rice wine vinegar
1	tablespoon sesame oil
2	teaspoons grated ginger

Prepare the udon noodles according to package directions. Set aside to drain and cool. In a 12-inch sauté pan over medium heat, sauté mushrooms with olive oil and lemon juice. Season with salt and pepper. Add spinach to wilt. Pour mixture into a large bowl to cool.

To make the dressing, bring mirin to a gentle boil in a small saucepan and add sugar and dashi. Bring to a boil again and add soy sauce; bring to a boil again and then remove from heat. Pour mixture into a jar and add rice vinegar, sesame oil, and ginger. Chill for at least two hours in refrigerator.

Add daikon and udon noodles to the mushroom mixture; toss with dressing. Garnish with shiso, ginger and nori.

Serves 4.

*Dashi-no-mono is an instant Japanese soup stock made from dried kelp (dashi konbu) and dried bonito (katsuo-bushi) and comes in a jar or packet in granular form. It can be found in the Asian food section of most markets.

STRAWBERRIES

S trawberries are grown on the slopes of Haleakalā on Maui and in
    Kamuela on the Big Island, where cooler temperatures provide an
    ideal growing environment.

Look for strawberries that are firm. The red color should go all the way
up to the tip. If the fruit is white by the green leaf, it means the farmer has
not let the fruit ripen far enough on the vine, producing a less sweet straw-
berry. Strawberries will not continue to ripen after being picked. Smaller
berries have a bit more flavor; larger ones are a bit watery.

Strawberries need to be refrigerated. Depending on the shape that the
berries are in when purchased, they will usually hold up for a good week to
a week and a half.

Eat strawberries raw and uncooked. They are also delicious in a cob-
bler, but they lose quite a bit of volume when cooked. Strawberries can be
frozen, but when defrosted they will lose their shape. If freezing, use within
six months.

MEASURING STRAWBERRIES

1½ pounds = 2 pints or 1 quart	1 pint = 2¼ cups sliced berries
1 small basket = 1 pint	1 pint = 1⅔ cup pureed berries
1 pint = 3¼ cups whole berries	1 cup = approximately 4 ounces

Strawberry Lemon Shortbread with Ginger Cream
Teresa Shurilla, Maui Community College

2   pints strawberries
2   tablespoons white raw sugar*
    Confectioner's sugar for garnishing

GINGER CREAM
2   cups heavy cream
½   cup sugar
1   tablespoon fresh ginger, peeled and chopped
6   egg yolks, beaten

LEMON SHORTBREAD
¾   cup unsalted butter
½   cup granulated sugar
1   egg yolk
2   tablespoons heavy cream
½   teaspoon vanilla extract
2   cups cake flour, sifted
½   teaspoon salt
    Zest of 1 lemon

Strawberries are sometimes very dirty, but should not be soaked because they tend to weep. Fill a bowl with water, dump the berries in, move them around and pull them out immediately with a mesh strainer. Depending on the size, cut in quarters, sprinkle with sugar and set aside.

To make the ginger cream, place the cream, sugar, and ginger in a stainless saucepan. Bring to boil, turn off heat and let mixture steep for 20 minutes. Bring mixture back to a boil, remove from the heat and pour slowly over the egg yolks, whisking constantly. Return mixture back to the heat and cook over medium heat for three to five minutes until it thickens.

Strain the entire mixture through a fine mesh strainer. Cool the custard by placing the bowl over ice or placing in refrigerator uncovered. The cream needs at least four hours to set; overnight is preferable.

To make the lemon shortbread, preheat oven to 325° F.

Cream butter and sugar. Add egg yolk, cream, vanilla extract and zest and blend well. Blend the flour and salt in by hand and form a ball. Wrap and refrigerate for a couple hours.

Remove the dough from the refrigerator and knead for a couple minutes to soften. Roll the dough to approximately a quarter of an inch thick and cut with a three-inch cookie cutter, allowing two pieces per person. Place on a parchment-lined baking sheet. Bake for 25 minutes or until the edges of the pastry are a light golden brown. Remove from oven and cool on a rack.

To serve, place a cookie on the plate and spoon about half a cup of berries on top of the cookie. Layer with a scoop of ginger cream, top with another cookie, dust with powdered sugar and serve immediately.

Serves 8.

White raw sugar is a natural sugar, less refined than granulated sugar and contains a little molasses. It is a Maui-grown and -processed product available at supermarkets throughout the state.

Lemon Pannacotta with Balsamic Strawberries
Teresa Shurilla, Maui Community College

5   teaspoons powdered gelatin or 5 sheets gelatin
½   cup cold water
1½ cups heavy cream
⅔   cup granulated sugar
1   tablespoon finely chopped lemon zest
1¼ cups buttermilk

BALSAMIC STRAWBERRIES
2   pints of strawberries, washed and sliced
1   tablespoon balsamic vinegar
6   tablespoons white raw sugar*

Bloom (dissolve) the gelatin by putting the water in a bowl and sprinkling the gelatin on top; let stand for 5 minutes.

Meanwhile, heat the cream, sugar and zest in a saucepan to about 180° F. Stir in gelatin and allow to cool to lukewarm. Stir in buttermilk and blend well. Pour into six 10-ounce soufflé cups, custard dishes, or wine glasses. Refrigerate for three to four hours or until set. Garnish with the fresh strawberries and a sprig of mint.

Toss strawberries with balsamic and sugar just before serving. If the process is done too early you will not get the crunch of the sugar. Spoon on top of the pannacotta and serve.

Serves 6.

White raw sugar is a natural sugar, less refined than granulated sugar and contains a little molasses. It is a Maui-grown and -processed product available at supermarkets throughout the state.

Chauncy Monden, Kula Country Farms
Kula, Maui

When you've been farming since you were five years old, it's hard to do anything else. With that lifelong experience, a business degree and the desire to return to Maui to raise a family, farming seemed to be the right thing to do. So eight years ago, Chauncy Monden returned to his family farm, becoming the fourth generation to farm in Kula, Maui.

He wanted to grow something different and create brand recognition for a product. He chose strawberries, a crop well suited to the cold nights and warm days of Upcountry Maui. With 12 to 15 acres of strawberries, planted in three cycles, Kula Country Farms is producing some of the sweetest berries grown in Hawai'i.

The high costs of land, labor and water all impact the ability of local farmers to compete with products shipped to Maui, says Monden. "But it's gratifying to be able to produce a consistent product. The beginning of the planting cycle is the best time – you're hopeful and optimistic that the harvest will be bountiful and the produce superior."

SWEET POTATO

Homegrown sweet potatoes, mostly from Moloka'i and Maui, are delicious, sweet and versatile as ingredients in side dishes, snacks and desserts. The Okinawan variety, a vivid purple, is popular in the Islands for its striking color and sweetness.

When buying sweet potatoes, look for smooth, unbruised skin that is firm and fresh looking; avoid mold, soft spots or broken areas. Purchase potatoes of the same size to allow for even cooking.

Store sweet potatoes in a cool, dark place. Refrigeration will convert the starch to sugar and alter the texture. Sweet potatoes can be stored for two months under optimal conditions.

Don't peel or boil sweet potatoes, as they lose much of their flavor. Roasting will intensify the flavor. In supermarkets, sweet potatoes are displayed next to yams, which are actually just a variety of sweet potatoes, a moister variant with a darker skin.

Purple Sweet Potato Poke   *Good)*
Lori Wong, Culinary Consultant

Serve this as an appetizer or salad. The vibrant color will be a feast for the eyes.

2   pounds purple sweet potatoes, roasted and peeled
1   small sweet onion, sliced
1   stalk green onions, minced ← *sub corn*
¼   cup any soy sauce-based dressing

Dice sweet potatoes into ½-inch cubes. Toss with onion, green onions and dressing.
Serves 6 to 8.

Sweet Potato Flan
Sabine Glissmann, Halekulani Hotel

2   cups sweet potatoes, peeled and chopped
1½   cups half and half
2   eggs
1   egg yolk
     salt and pepper to taste

Preheat oven to 325° F. Lightly oil six 5-ounce ramekins.
In a saucepan, combine sweet potatoes with half and half. Bring to a boil over medium heat; then reduce heat to a simmer and cook until sweet potatoes are tender. Remove from heat and cool. Transfer to a food processor and puree. Add eggs and yolk. Season to taste; pulse to blend well. Pour into ramekins.
Place ramekins in a shallow pan filled with an inch of water. Bake for 40 minutes or until flan mixture is firm. Let stand for 10 minutes. With a sharp paring knife, loosen the flan from the ramekin to release. Serve warm.
Serves 6.

Okinawan Sweet Potato Macadamia Nut Pie

Lori Wong, Culinary Consultant

This striking purple pie is remarkable, and the texture, after refrigeration, is like a cheesecake.

1¼   pound Okinawan sweet potatoes, roasted, peeled and cubed
1¼   cups vanilla yogurt
¾   cups dark brown sugar, packed
½   teaspoon ground cinnamon
¼   teaspoon freshly ground nutmeg
5   eggs, beaten
1   (9-inch) deep dish frozen pie shell, room temperature
1   cup macadamia nuts, chopped
1   tablespoon maple syrup
     Dash salt

Preheat oven to 350° F.

In a food processor, process sweet potatoes until creamy. Add yogurt, brown sugar, cinnamon, nutmeg, salt, and eggs. Pulse until all ingredients are well combined. Pour mixture into pie shell. Toss macadamia nuts with maple syrup. Sprinkle nuts over the top.

Bake for 55 minutes or until a knife inserted into pie comes out clean. Remove from the oven and cool on a rack. Refrigerate.

Yields one 9-inch pie.

Lynn and Russell DeCoite, L & R Farms
Hoʻolehua, Molokaʻi

Lynn Mokuau DeCoite was the odd one out among her brothers and sisters: the only one who never wanted to leave Molokaʻi to go to Kamehameha Schools, the only one who didn't mind her hands in the dirt. She loved farming and knew she would carry on in her parents' and grandparents' tradition. It was a proud tradition. After all, wasn't the Mokuau variety of Molokaʻi sweet potato named for her grandmother, Becky?

Lynn and her husband, Russell, now operate L & R Farms, growing Molokaʻi purple and Molokaʻi gold sweet potatoes on 200 leased acres in the central Hoʻolehua plains. Russell DeCoite grew up ranching so he understood, as Lynn did, that it would be a hard life, one ruled more than they like by the weather, but a good one, too. They have three children ages 10, 9, and 6, all of whom have helped with planting, harvesting, weeding. "They have done it all and they know the ins and outs," says Lynn DeCoite proudly.

In fact, they're one reason for her philosophy that, in farming, you have to be willing to change. The children had a good idea about mixing different colors of potatoes in the chips they make for sale on Molokaʻi, adding something unique to their brand. Like many farmers, she's found that producing a value-added product (something processed, like the chips) helps the bottom line. "You change with the times or you're out of the game," she says.

TARO

Taro came to Hawaiʻi with the earliest Polynesian settlers in their canoes and has been cultivated intensely on the leeward coasts of all the major Hawaiian islands. In the early days, there were more than 300 varieties of taro; approximately 87 of these varieties are recognizable today, with slight differences in height, stalk, color, leaf or flower color, size, and root type. Some of the local varieties are Moʻi, Lehua, Haʻakea and Chinese.

Taro, a hearty succulent perennial herb, is cultivated both in the uplands – as high as 4,000 feet – and in marshy land irrigated by streams. Depending on the variety, all parts of this sturdy and hardy plant are eaten. The leaves, known as lūʻau, are cooked as greens, similar to spinach, and are high in vitamins and minerals. The tubers are eaten baked, boiled or steamed, or cooked and mashed with water to make poi. The fibrous flesh of the tuber is tough and spongy, ranging in color from white or yellow to blue-purple to pink or reddish. Most important is the starchy root with enough glutinosity to make quality poi, the soul food of Hawai'i. Taro is often fed to babies as their first whole and natural healthy food, as well as to the elderly, for its ease of digestion and high vitamin content.

When buying taro, look for clean corms that are fully developed, as opposed to knobby or diseased-looking ones. Become familiar with different varieties and seek advice from the farmer/vendors.

Store taro in the refrigerator. In optimal conditions (cool, dry and dark) fresh taro can be stored for two months. Freezing is not advisable.

Important: before taro can be eaten, all parts of the plant must be cooked, in order to break down the needle-like calcium oxalate crystals present in the leaves, stem and corm. These could be extremely irritating to the throat and mouth lining, causing an acrid burning and stinging sensation.

To prepare taro, steam or bake whole and unpeeled for best flavor. After cooking, remove skin and slice or dice to serving size. Pound to make poi, or eat like a potato with butter.

Taro, Sweet Potato and 'Ulu Salad
Lori Wong, Culinary Consultant

A really colorful and versatile salad.

1   cup Chinese taro, cooked and cut into 1-inch cubes
1   cup Okinawan (purple) sweet potato, cooked and cut into 1-inch cubes
1   cup golden sweet potato, cooked and cut into 1-inch cubes
1   cup breadfruit ('ulu), cooked and cut into 1-inch cubes
2   stalks green onions, finely chopped
½   cup celery, diced
½   cup sweet onions, sliced
1   teaspoon Hawaiian salt
1   teaspoon ground pepper
¼   teaspoon cayenne pepper
½   cup of your favorite salad dressing

Combine all ingredients in a large bowl and toss to combine. Serves 4.

Rodney Haraguchi, W. T. Haraguchi Farm
Hanalei, Kaua'i

"I like the country, the open feeling, the independence," says Rodney Haraguchi, a fourth-generation farmer who has grown rice and truck crops and is now one of the largest producers of wetland taro. Like every farmer, Haraguchi faces his share of challenges: water supply, adequate labor force and battling a voracious pest, the apple snail. "We just have to take them one at a time."

Haraguchi has been working on the farm his whole life and is pleased that his daughter Lyndsey and her husband Brad Nakayama are now helping to run the 80-plus-year-old farm. "My father and grandfather gave me the experience of hard work and commitment to the land," says Haraguchi, and he now looks forward to enjoying the fruits of his labor.

Kaua'i Taro Patties
Kaua'i Farm Bureau

Place two patties on a bed of fresh salad greens and drizzle with dressing. Use as a base for smoked salmon with a touch of sour cream for an appetizer.

1   pound Chinese taro, cooked and mashed
2   tablespoons butter
1   small sweet onion, diced
2   cloves garlic, minced
2   stalks green onions, thinly sliced
1   teaspoon Hawaiian salt
⅔   cup heavy cream
2   tablespoons lemon juice
⅓   cup cornstarch
1   tablespoons baking powder
2   tablespoons fresh basil, chopped
    Oil for frying

Melt butter in a skillet over medium-high heat. Add the onions, garlic and green onion and sauté for two to three minutes. Combine mashed taro, heavy cream, lemon juice, cornstarch, baking powder, basil and salt and blend well. Add onion mixture and shape into eight patties and refrigerate for 30 minutes.

Heat oil in a skillet and fry patties until crisp.

Serves 4.

TOMATO

Tomatoes can be grown year-round in Hawai‘i, though summer is still "their" time. Unless you are growing your own, the best place to get a tomato is at a farmers market, where a vine-ripened delight with a true tomato flavor can be counted on.

There are many varieties grown by Island farmers, including heirloom varieties. Try them all: yellow, zebra, orange, pear, green (some types are actually ripe when green), etc. Typically, the yellow and orange tend to have the least acid, but talk to the farmer and have him or her describe the flavor and how they can best be used.

One of the most important things to know about tomatoes is that you should never refrigerate them: that will kill the flavor. Store them stem-side-up on your counter and use when soft to the touch and aromatic.

More tips for enjoying tomatoes:

• Slice them and serve simply with a little salt and pepper – their own flavor is great unadorned.

• Buy as many different colors and types as possible and alternately layer the colors in a spiral on a plate.

• Drizzle with extra-virgin olive oil and balsamic vinegar and salt and pepper.

• Add sliced fresh buffalo mozzarella in between a few of the tomato slices and top with a chiffonade of basil.

• Add a finely chopped and seeded tomato to your scrambled eggs like they do in France.

• Combine chopped fresh tomatoes with fresh basil, lots of chopped garlic, extra-virgin olive oil, salt and pepper and toss with freshly cooked fettuccine and serve immediately. You can also top toasted bread slices with this tomato mixture.

• Peel a tomato by dropping it into a pot of boiling water for a few seconds. Remove and cool, then slide off the skins. To remove the seeds, just cut in half and squeeze out them out.

Fresh Tomato Salsa
Beverly Gannon, Hali'imaile General Store

Use really good ripe tomatoes for this salsa; serve it with chips or 'Ulu Crackers. Add some chopped salted salmon and replace the cilantro with green onion to make lomi salmon. Or replace the cilantro with flat leaf parsley and serve it atop grilled bread for a terrific bruschetta. It's the tomatoes that count!

2   cups chopped tomatoes
¼   cup chopped sweet onion
1   teaspoon minced garlic, about 1 clove
¼   cup chopped cilantro
1   chili pepper, minced
1   teaspoon Hawaiian salt

Combine all ingredients in a bowl. Let the flavors mingle for about 30 minutes and serve at room temperature.
Makes about 2½ cups.

Roasted Tomatoes
Maria Tucker, Aloha Gourmet

This is a great side dish for dinner – roasting really brings out the flavor of the tomato. You can also sprinkle with fine breadcrumbs and/or Parmesan cheese during the last five minutes for an added treat.

8 to 10   tomatoes
1   tablespoon extra-virgin olive oil
½   teaspoon fresh thyme, basil, chervil or marjoram
½   teaspoon sea salt
¼   teaspoon freshly ground black or white pepper

Preheat oven to 425° F.

Slice tomatoes in half, place in a bowl and toss with the remaining ingredients. Arrange in a single layer with the cut sides up and bake about 30 minutes.

Serves 6.

WATERCRESS

Spicy, crunchy watercress is especially delicious in Hawai'i. There are about a dozen watercress farms on O'ahu; the largest, Sumida Farms, Inc. in 'Aiea, supplies about 70 percent of the fresh watercress market.

Select watercress bunches that are bright green and crisp. Cut off the stems an inch or two from the bottom and rinse the whole bunch in a large bowl of cool water. Drain well and refrigerate in a plastic bag, or place the stems in a container of water, cover the tops with a plastic bag and refrigerate. Watercress will keep for four to five days, after which the leaves will start to yellow.

Watercress is good raw as a salad, with or without other greens, or added to sandwiches for crunch and a peppery bite. It is also excellent in soups, pureed into a sauce or simply sautéed. To prepare, simply pick off the tops and the next two or three sprigs down, saving the lower stems for cooking, or just cut the whole bunch into desired lengths.

Watercress is rich in vitamins A, C and B1. It's also a good source of iron, potassium, phosphorous, calcium and fiber and contains isothiocyanate, which is good for the lungs, and lutein for healthy eyes. The Chinese brew a "tea" from the stems that is a tonic for a host of symptoms.

Watercress Salad with Roasted Beets, Candied Walnuts & Liliko'i Balsamic Vinaigrette
Barbara Potts, Maui County Farm Bureau

SALAD
2	bunches watercress, tough stems removed
3	medium beets with stems removed
4	cups mixed baby greens
1	small sweet onion, thinly sliced
¼	cup crumbled goat cheese

CANDIED WALNUTS
½	cup walnuts
2	tablespoons butter
2	tablespoons brown sugar

DRESSING
2	liliko'i
¼	cup balsamic vinegar
¼	cup sugar
1	teaspoon Dijon mustard
1	teaspoon salt
½	small sweet onion
1	cup canola oil

Scrub the beets, rub with a little oil, season with salt and wrap in foil. Roast in a 375°F oven for about an hour or until tender when pierced with a knife. Cool, peel and slice into wedges. Refrigerate.

To make the walnuts, brown them in butter. Add brown sugar, stir constantly until sugar melts and caramelizes. Turn mixture onto waxed paper to cool.

To make the dressing, scoop the contents of the liliko'i, seeds and all, into a blender (a blender will grind the liliko'i seeds better than a food processor). Add sugar, mustard, salt and onion and pulse until blended. With the motor running, slowly add the oil; blend until mixture is thick and well blended. Chill the dressing.

In a large bowl, toss together the watercress, baby greens and Maui onion with a small amount of dressing. Divide among six plates; arrange beets on top of greens. Sprinkle with walnuts and goat cheese. Drizzle more dressing on top. Serve at once.

Serves 6.

Watercress Tempura
David Sumida's grandmother's recipe

1   bunch watercress
½   cup plus 1 tablespoon flour
½   cup less 1 tablespoon cornstarch
1   tablespoon salt
1   large egg
     Vegetable oil for deep-frying

Combine dry ingredients in a bowl. Beat egg in a measuring cup and add enough water to make ¾ cup. Add to the dry ingredients and mix until just combined. Do not over-beat.

Chill the batter in the refrigerator for at least one hour before using. Meanwhile, wash and dry the watercress and cut into one-inch lengths.

In a deep saucepan or wok, heat about two inches of oil to 375° F. Mix the watercress into the batter. Drop the mixture by tablespoons onto the hot oil and flatten the patties slightly. Fry until golden brown, turn and cook the other side. Drain on paper towels and serve immediately.

Serves 6 as an appetizer or side dish.

Sautéed Watercress
Noreen Lam

Eat this simply sautéed watercress as a side dish or combine it with pasta.

1   bunch watercress, cut in 2-inch lengths
2-3 cloves garlic, peeled and thinly sliced
1   tablespoon olive oil
1   tablespoon soy sauce
    Pinch red pepper flakes
    Extra-virgin lemon olive oil

Heat olive oil in a large sauté pan over medium-high heat. Add the garlic slices and cook until light golden, being careful not to let them burn. Add the watercress, soy sauce, and red pepper flakes. Toss and cook until the watercress is just wilted. Remove from the heat and drizzle with the lemon oil.

Serves 4.

Watercress Salad with Soba Noodles and Tofu
Noreen Lam, former chef, Contemporary Museum Café

1   bunch watercress, washed, dried and cut into 2-inch lengths
2   bundles soba noodles
1   (14-ounce) block firm tofu
2   cups fresh bean sprouts (optional)
1   medium Japanese cucumber, halved, seeded and sliced diagonally, ¼-inch thick
12   grape or cherry tomatoes
2   green onions, sliced diagonally, for garnish
     Toasted sesame seeds

GARLIC-SOY DRESSING
½   cup low-sodium soy sauce
2   tablespoons sugar
¼   cup vegetable oil
2   cloves garlic, thinly sliced
1   tablespoon ginger, cut into fine julienne

Cook soba noodles in boiling water for three to four minutes, being careful not to overcook them. Drain and rinse in cold water until cool. Drain well and toss with a little oil to prevent them from sticking together.

Drain tofu to remove excess water. Cut into cubes.

Combine soy sauce and sugar; stir until sugar dissolves. Heat oil in a small saucepan, add the garlic and cook over medium heat until the garlic is light golden. Add the ginger and cook a few seconds longer. Remove from the heat and add the soy mixture. Stir to combine and set aside.

Place the watercress in a large bowl or platter and add bean sprouts if desired. Mound the soba noodles in the center. Scatter the tofu, cucumber and tomatoes around. Remix the dressing and pour over the salad. Garnish with the green onions and sesame seeds.

For a non-vegetarian option, add to or replace tofu with sliced kamaboko, char siu, or egg sheets.

Serves 4-6.

ZUCCHINI

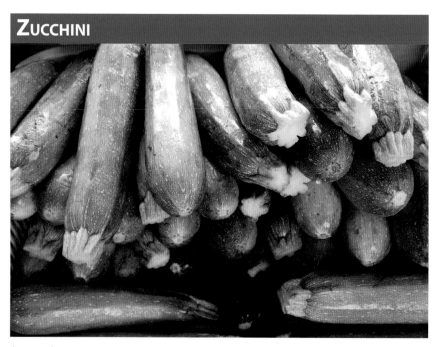

T he most popular of the summer squash, zucchini has a delicately
light flavor beneath its light to dark green skin. Choose small to
medium squash, which have thinner skins and more tender flesh.
Look for unblemished skin that is vibrant in color. Zucchini can be cooked
in a number of ways: steamed, grilled, sautéed, deep-fried or baked. You
can even eat zucchini raw: using a slicer, cut zucchini into thin lengthwise
ribbons and simply dress with olive oil, lemon juice and salt and pepper for
a simply delicious salad.

Zucchini Flan

Tish Uyehara, Armstrong Produce

6   zucchini, coarsely chopped
4   tablespoons butter or olive oil
½   cup cream
2   eggs
    Freshly grated nutmeg*

Preheat oven to 300° F. Butter six ramekins or custard cups.

Heat butter or oil in a sauté pan over medium-high heat. Add zucchini and sauté about five minutes until tender. Season with salt and pepper. Remove from heat and cool. When zucchini is cool, squeeze out as much liquid as possible.

Mix zucchini with cream and eggs. Divide mixture among ramekins and place in a baking pan. Fill pan with warm water halfway up the sides of the ramekins. Bake for 15 to 20 minutes or until custard is set. Remove from oven and serve warm.

Serves 6 as a side dish.

Fresh nutmeg is grown in Hawai'i and is often available at farmers markets. It is usually sold with the lacy membrane surrounding the nut that is called mace. Use a fine grater for whole nutmeg and enjoy its warm, spicy and sweet aroma.

Zucchini Juhn

Joan Namkoong, Freelance Food Writer

One of the simplest and tastiest ways to prepare zucchini is Korean-style, as juhn. Simply coated in flour, dipped in egg and quickly fried, zucchini juhn is easy to prepare and delicious.

2 zucchini, cut into 3/8-inch slices
½ cup all purpose flour
2 eggs, beaten
   Salt to taste
   Oil for frying

Coat slices of zucchini with flour – the easiest way is to put zucchini and flour in a plastic bag, close bag and shake. Dip each flour-coated slice in beaten egg.

In a large skillet over high heat, heat two to three tablespoons of oil. When the oil is hot, place slices of zucchini in pan, sprinkle with salt and fry, about two minutes per side. Zucchini should be golden brown and tender when pierced with a fork, but still firm. Remove from pan and drain on paper towels. Serve warm or at room temperature.

You can serve zucchini juhn with a dipping sauce of equal parts of soy sauce and rice vinegar.

Serves 6.

Photo Credits

The Hawai'i Farm Bureau and Les Dames d'Escoffier would like to thank the following photographers for their time spent capturing each product in its best light – from visiting various farmlands to perusing the open markets, their contributions truly highlight some of the best Hawai'i has to offer:

Big Island Farm Bureau
Brian Miyamoto
Dawn Sakamoto
Faith Ogawa
Hayley Matson-Mathes
Hawai'i Department of Agriculture
Howard Yamasaki
Joan Namkoong
Karol Haraguchi
Kauai County Farm Bureau
Ken Love
Lorie Farell
Lynn DeCoite
Michael Mathes
Miles Hakoda
Nicole Chew
Richard Ha
Sue Keller
College of Tropical Agriculture and Human Resources,
      University of Hawai'i at Mānoa
Valerie Kaneshiro

Hawai'i Fruits Seasonality Chart

M - Indicates MODERATE availability
P - Indicates PEAK availability

	JAN	FEB	MAR	APR	MAY	JUN	JUL	AUG	SEP	OCT	NOV	DEC
Atemoya	M	M						M	M	P	P	P
Avocado	P	P	M	M				M	M		P	P
Banana	M	M	M	M	M	P	P	P	P	P	M	M
Cantaloupe					M	P	P	P	M			
Honeydew					M	P	P	P	M			
Lime	P	P	P			P	P	P	P	P	P	P
Longan	M	M	M	M	M	M	M	P	P	P	M	M
Lychee	M	M	M	M	P	P	P	P	P	M	M	M
Mango		P	P	P	P	P	P	P	P	P	P	
Orange	P	P	P	P	M	M	M	M	P	P	P	P
Papaya	M	M	P	P	P	P	P	P	P	P	P	M
Persimmon									P	P	M	
Pineapple	M	M	M	P	P	P	P	P	P	M	M	M
Rambutan	P	P	P							P	P	P
Strawberry	P	P	P	P	M	M	M			M	M	M
Starfruit	M	M	M	M					M	M	M	M
Tangerine	P	M								M	P	P
Watermelon					M	P	P	P	P	M		

Source: Hawai'i Agriculture & Food Products Directory • www.Hawaiiag.org/hdoa/

Hawai'i Vegetables Seasonality Chart

M - Indicates MODERATE availability
P - Indicates PEAK availability

	JAN	FEB	MAR	APR	MAY	JUN	JUL	AUG	SEP	OCT	NOV	DEC
Beans	M	M	M	P	P	P	P	P	M	M	M	M
Bittermelon	M	P	P	P	P	P	M	M				
Burdock	M	M	M					M	P	P	P	P
Cabbage, Chinese	P	P	P	P	P	P	P	P	M	M	M	M
Cabbage, Head	M	P	P	P	P	P	M	M	M	M	M	M
Cabbage, Asian	M	M	M				M	P	P	P	P	P
Celery		M	M	P	P	P	P	P	M	M		
Corn, Sweet	M	P	P	P	P	P	M	M	M	M	P	P
Cucumber	M	M	M	P	P	P	P	P	M	M	M	M
Daikon	M	M	M	M	M	M	P	P	P	P	M	M
Eggplant	M	M	P	P	P	P	M	M	M	M	M	M
Ginger Root		M	M	P	P	P	P	P	M	M		
Heart of Palm	P	P	P	P	P	P	P	P	P	P	P	P
Herbs	M	M	M	M	M	M	M	M	M	M	M	M
Lettuce, Baby Greens	M	M	M				M	M	P	P	P	P
Lettuce, Romaine	M	M	M	M	M	P	P	P	P	M	M	M
Lettuce, Leaf	M	M	P	P	P	P	P	M	M	M	M	M
Lū'au (Taro) Leaf				M	M	P	P	P	M	M		
Mushrooms	P	P	P	P	P	P	P	P	P	P	P	P
Onion, Round			M	P	P	P	P	P	M	M		
Onion, Green	M	M	M	M	M	M	P	P	P	P	M	M
Parsley, American	M	M	P	P	P	P	M	M				
Pepper, Green	M	M	M	P	P	P	P	P	M	M	M	M
Potato, Sweet	M	P	P	P	P	P	M	M				
Pumpkin	M	M	M			M	M	P	P	P	P	P
Sprouts	P	P	P	P	P	P	P	P	P	P	P	P
Squash				M	M	P	P	P	P	M	M	
Taro	M	M	P	P	P	P	P	M	M	M	P	P
Tomato	M	M	M	M	P	P	P	P	P	P	M	M
Zucchini	M	M	M			M	M	P	P	P	P	P

Source: Hawai'i Agriculture & Food Products Directory • www.Hawaiiag.org/hdoa/

Index of Recipes

Index of Products